D1267505

SELLING OUT?
Privatisation in Ireland
by Paul Sweeney October 2004

AFTER THE BALL
by Fintan O'Toole October 2003

www.stmichaelsestate.ie.

Regeneration
Public Good or Private Profit?

JOHN BISSETT

To Shanley

Thanks for your support and inspiration

John Bissett

2009.

Regeneration
First published 2008
by tasc at New Island
an imprint of New Island Press
2 Brookside
Dundrum
Dublin 14

www.newisland.ie

ISBN 978-1-905494-91-0

British Library Cataloguing in Publication Data.
A CIP catalogue record for this book is available
from the British Library.

Typeset by Ashfield Press
Cover design by Public Communications Centre

Printed in Ireland by
Betaprint Limited, Dublin

Contents

TASC would like to acknowledge with gratitude the
financial contribution to this publication of the
Equality Studies Centre
at the UCD School of Social Justice.

ABOUT THE AUTHOR

JOHN BISSETT was born in Dolphin House, Rialto, a social housing complex in Dublin. He served an apprenticeship as a fitter in the Irish Glass Bottle Company in the early 1980s. He is a graduate of National University of Ireland Maynooth with a degree in Sociology and English. He continued his studies in University College Dublin and was awarded a Masters and Ph.D. in Sociology on the same occasion in 2001. John currently works as a Community Worker for the Canal Communities Local Drugs Task Force in Dublin. He has been a member of the St. Michael's Estate Community Regeneration Team since February 2001. He is married to Grainne Lord and they have three children, Laoise, Kara and Zoe.

Single is the race, single
Of men and of gods;
From a single mother we both draw breath.
But a difference of power in everything
Keeps us apart.
(The Greek Poet, Pindar, 5th Century BC[1])

It takes a lot of things to change the world:
Anger and tenacity, science and indignation,
The quick initiative, the long reflection,
The cold patience and the infinite perseverance,
The understanding of the particular case and the understanding of
the ensemble,
Only the lessons of reality can teach us to transform reality.
(Bertolt Brecht.[2])

Acknowledgements

There are a number of people and organisations without whose support this book would never have seen the light of day.

This book truly belongs to my hard working colleagues on St. Michael's Estate Community Regeneration Team and the people who live in St. Michael's Estate. This book was born out of a need to understand what regeneration meant for the people involved in it. The Regeneration Team wanted to understand and articulate what exactly regeneration meant – who benefits most, who gets what and at what cost, who gets listened to and who doesn't? They knew that it wasn't quite what it said on the tin. So the idea of thinking, talking and writing about the regeneration process of the Estate was hugely supported. The Team had a good instinct that St. Michael's Estate provided an opportunity for a piece of research that mattered to people and could make a difference. This book is a community account of urban regeneration. It charts the intense struggle and hard work that took place to ensure that the residents of St. Michael's Estate had a voice in the development of their homes, community and local environment.

This book gives us a voice and a chance to be heard. We hope it will be an educational tool for everyone involved in regeneration and Public Private Partnership. It is our aim that future projects will learn from this book and build on our experience and ensure that the process of regeneration is improved and developed in the interests of the people who live in the area. This is our story, written from our experience and perspective. It is an honest account of what it is like for working class people to engage with the process of regeneration – a group that have few resources, no funding, little networking capacity but have determination, ambition, community spirit, and powerful camaraderie. It is difficult to put into words the trials and triumphs of drawing up a regeneration plan with the residents' interests at the forefront, within the restrictive framework of Public Private Partnership (PPP).

Undoubtedly, there are many different perspectives on the process and happenings that have taken place over the last few years. This is only one account among many and I am sure that there are people who may not agree with every word. However, this is our account and this book charts the last seven years of our involvement in the regeneration process. It documents meetings, protests, presentations, focus groups, consultations, media coverage, obstacles and dialogue that has gotten us to where we are today. It is important that people are encouraged and are free to write or to talk about their stories of the process of regeneration as much as we have here. We welcome dialogue with contrasting viewpoints on regeneration. Such dialogue undoubtedly enriches our understanding of what is in fact a very complex process.

The following people have worked unselfishly on the Community Regeneration Team for all, or part of the past seven years: Eilish Comerford, Sister Jo Kennedy, Rita Fagan, Michael O Flanagan, Gerry Mc Dermott, the late, great Linda Kavanagh, Martin Carroll, Celine Martin, Natasha Farrell, Caroline Mc Nulty, Nikki Fahey, Rose Martin, Nicole Green, Sister Mary Stafford, Jim Doyle and Sinead Clancy.

In 2005 while struggling with how to make sense of what was happening in St. Michael's Estate I approached Professor Kathleen Lynch in the Equality Studies Centre, School of Social Justice, University College Dublin, with a very rough, early draft of written material. Since that time she has provided invaluable support and a staunch sense of solidarity with this project. The Equality Studies Centre generously provided funding for me to take a short sabbatical to go to UCD and work undisturbed on this project. The staff and students of the Equality Studies Centre also participated in presentations and seminars on this work. At different times all of the staff in the Equality Studies Centre helped with this project. Thanks to Maureen Lyons, John Baker, Judy Walsh, Sara Cantillon, Pauline Faughnan, Elizabeth Hassell and Niall O'Hanlon. Without this structured time to think, reflect and to write, the book would probably remain an unfinished paper going round in circles. Mimi Doran, a Ph.D. student in Equality Studies also provided the Regeneration Team with excellent media training and advice on the publication and launch of this book.

One of our desperate failings in community work in recent years has been our inability to publish and distribute material we have produced. In the publication of this work we have been very fortunate to have linked up with TASC who have been producing and disseminating work of a very high standard for many years now. Their expertise has proved invaluable in getting this book out to the public and we very much appreciate the time, effort and commitment of Paula Clancy, Eithne MacManus and Kay Garvey.

There are many groups and agencies that need to be acknowledged and thanked for their contribution to the regeneration process: On St. Michael's Estate Task Force there have been a number of Chairs in recent years, including Senator Brendan Ryan, the late Michael Mc Donnell, Fintan Farrell and especially Maria Hegarty who chaired the Task Force through very difficult times and helped lay the foundations for the new Regeneration Board; Trish Brennan, for her work on the Estate over the years; those who have/are participating on the new Regeneration Board, Chairperson Finbarr Flood, Carol Larkin, City Councillors Catherine Byrne, John Gallagher, Michael Connaghton, Criona Ni Dhalaigh and Claire Byrne, Michael Challoner from the local VEC; from Dublin City Council Brendan Kenny, Mary Taylor, Sean Smith, Gerry Folen and Michael O Neill; from the community Sector, Natasha Farrell, Caroline Mc Nulty, Nikki Fahey, Rita Fagan, Eilish Comerford, Celine Martin, Gerry Mc Dermott, Michael O' Flanagan, Luke Shanahan, Mary Fagan, Derek Bunyan, Marja Almqvist and John Byrnes from the Canal

Communities Partnership. To Sara Bermingham, Tony Smithers and Trevor in Dublin City Council's Estate Office in Goldenbridge, to Eadaoin Ni Chleirigh, Chief Executive of the Board, Catherine Cahill, Sinead Murphy, Catherine Farrell, Kay Ann O'Mahony and Dervla Masterson and the architectural team in Dublin City Council, thanks to all of you for your hard work and dedication.

My own organisation, The Canal Communities Local Drugs Task Force has shown great flexibility and understanding in the growth and development of this work. This Task Force has worked from a broader community development philosophy since its inception and this is due in no small part to its major driving force since it was set up, Tony Mac Carthaigh. Thanks to Mary Ryder for her support as co-ordinator of the Task Force and to my colleagues Trish O Neill, Olivia Carr, Elaine Whelan, Michelle Lennon, Patricia Boyle, Cliodhna Fogarty and Paul Holdaway. Thanks are also due to my close working colleagues in Rialto Community Network, Ann Swords, Walter Bowden, Debbie Lynch, Julie Mc Carthy, Atinuke Diya, and Liz Carolan.

Thanks are also due to a number of community work students from St. Patrick's College Maynooth who contributed to this process while on placement, Linda Evans, Helen Lowery, Olivia O Brien, Margaret Crickley, Ndakengenra Aliane, Afusa Afarielgun and Paddy Mc Nicholl. Thanks to Fionnuala Rodgerson who has provided architectural support and excellent advice to the residents and community organisations in St. Michael's Estate.

To all of those who have been involved in the Tenants First grassroots organisation from all over Dublin and beyond and to those on the Tenants First Steering Group past and present, Lena Jordan, Rita Fagan, Eilish Comerford, Pat Gates, Christine Taylor, Danny Pender, Marie Harding, Charlie Hammond, Kate Brophy, Jim Lawlor, Tommy Coombes, Rory Herne, Joe Donohoe, Dorothy Walker and Michael Punch. Mick Rafferty and Patricia Mac Carthy (Community Technical Aid), Anna Quigley (Citywide) and Brian Dillon (Nexus), Cecilia Forestal

(Community Action Network) thanks and keep up the good work.

To John Sutton, Phil McCaughey, Daragh O Toole, Brendan Foreman, Charlie O Neill and all the staff in the Public Communications Centre, we appreciate the support you have given the community of St. Michael's Estate, not just on the campaign and the book, but on many other projects. I also want to thank Telcotec Ltd for sponsoring our website and Jane Cleary of digitalenvie.com for designing and constructing it. Some of the media were also supportive of our work and we do appreciate your help.

A number of people gave up valuable time to read and make comments on early drafts of this work. Thanks to Jim Lawlor, Joe Donohoe, Tony Mac Carthaigh, Brian Dillon, Dr. Michael Punch, Professor Kathleen Lynch, Dr. Mary Kelly and Walter Bowden. There are numerous other people (too many to mention) who helped in a variety of ways and I very much appreciate your help.

A big thank you goes to the residents of St Michael's Estate, your spirit and experiences are truly inspirational.

Finally I thank my family, Grainne, my beloved, and my three girls, Laoise, Kara and Zoe; you have listened to me go on and on about regeneration, without you I could never have done it. To Grainne's dad, David Lord, I'll have four copies for you. And finally, thanks to my mother Ann, sisters Julie and Laura and to Sean, Paul, Philip and Thomas.

To all who have been involved I value your time, energy, criticism and advice.

John Bissett

A Glossary of Key Terms

REGENERATION:

The term 'Regeneration' is conventionally taken to mean the *physical* transformation of an area. In 1998 when tenants agreed to the total demolition of the entire complex of St. Michael's Estate they expressed a stated preference for it to be replaced with a Dublin City Council housing scheme. This effectively meant the demolition of the entire complex and its replacement with a completely new development. However, in recent years it has been argued, especially by residents and community organisations that regeneration should attempt to deal with outstanding social issues in estates and flat complexes. In other words there should be an accompanying programme of *social regeneration* to parallel the physical transformation. The community sector in St. Michael's Estate argued that regeneration should concern itself with challenging and addressing patterns of inequality on the Estate. The most obvious of these have to do with education, employment, health, income etc. In a broad sense, therefore, regeneration is both a physical and a social process. The story in this book would suggest that different groups and organisations have clearly different interpretations and expectations with regard to both the process and outcomes of 'regeneration'.

PUBLIC PRIVATE PARTNERSHIP (PPP):

The Irish Government defines PPP as "… a contractual arrangement between the public and private sectors, with clear agreement on shared objectives, for the delivery of an asset or service that would otherwise have been provided through traditional public sector procurement"(www.ppp.gov.ie). Such a broad definition tells little of the detail as to how Public Private Partnerships actually work in practice.

REQUEST FOR QUALIFICATIONS (RFQ):

A Request for Qualifications, is the first stage whereby expressions of interest in the new development are sought from prospective bidders etc. In practice this means placing an advertisement for a PPP project in the national newspapers. It is a request for interested developers and consortia to state their interest and to present their qualifications and experience to take on such a piece of work. At the RFQ stage interested parties are given a general specification outline as to what is required in the project.

REQUEST FOR PROPOSALS (RFP):

The Request for Proposals follows the RFQ, and is a request to a group of short listed developers to present detailed plans for a PPP project. In the case of St. Michael's Estate the four short-listed bidders were given a detailed RFP document outlining what was essential to the bid. This RFP document included information on the required tenure mix, densities, heights, community and commercial facilities and specific design requirements. The document also included the criteria on which bids would be assessed in relation to finance, design and timescale.

ASSESSMENT PANEL:

As part of the formal PPP process an Assessment Panel is set up and allocated the task of choosing a 'Preferred Bidder' for the project. The panel evaluates all of the respective bids and plans and chooses one of them. In general these panels are comprised totally of 'professional experts'. In St. Michael's Estate the local tenants organisation rejected this view and insisted that there be community representation on the panel. This was eventually agreed to and two community representatives participated, along with the 'experts', in the choosing of a preferred bidder and a new masterplan for St. Michael's Estate.

SOCIAL HOUSING:

Social Housing is 'not for profit' housing that is managed and owned by the Irish State. The flats on St. Michael's Estate were managed by Dublin City Council on behalf of the State. In the past such housing was called 'public housing' and many tenants and participants within the regeneration process still use the term public when speaking of such housing.

AFFORDABLE HOUSING:

Housing purchased at the build cost of the house. In the metropolitan area of Dublin city these schemes are run and organised by Dublin City Council with a view to providing accommodation at a reasonable rate for those who cannot afford to buy on the open market.

FLATS:

Many people in Dublin and beyond still use the term 'flats' to refer to what have today become more commonly known as apartments. A 'flat' describes accommodation units built one on top of the other within buildings of variable heights. In the case of St. Michael's Estate the 'flats' referred to are the accommodation units within the two, four and eight storey buildings that were constructed in 1969-70. In the four and eight storey blocks for example, there were usually four flats on each level or floor.

Chronology of key dates and events in St. Michael's Estate

1970: The construction of St. Michael's Estate. The estate is in Inchicore, just over two miles from Dublin City centre. When built in 1970, the Estate comprised 346 flats in two, four and eight storey blocks scattered over eleven acres of land. In recent years, a number of the blocks have been demolished and many of the original residents have been housed either off site or in two adjacent schemes as part of the first phase of regeneration.

1985: The St. Michael's Estate Family Resource Centre is founded. This is a Community Development Project that supports local residents to get the best possible physical and social regeneration.

1986: The St. Michael's Estate Blocks' Committee is set up. This is the local residents' organisation with representatives coming from each of the blocks on the Estate. In the late 1980s, the Family Resource Centre sought funding for a community worker to support this group. The proposal was successful and this support has continued right up to the present.

1997: Establishment of the St. Michael's Estate Task Force. This was an integrated structure which was made up of members of the local Blocks' Committee, local community and voluntary projects, residents from an adjacent estate and statutory agencies. This group had a number of independent chairpersons and met on a monthly basis. In 1997, residents of the Estate anticipated a proposal from Dublin City Council for a refurbishment scheme for St. Michael's Estate which never materialised.

1998: St. Michael's Estate Task Force commissions a consultation document on the future of the Estate. Sixty-four per cent of local residents agree to the total demolition of the Estate. Residents recommend that a new City Council scheme replace the old, with traditional houses with front and back gardens.

1999: A draft regeneration plan is put forward for consideration by Dublin City Council. In response, the local League of Ireland football club, St. Patrick's Athletic, proposes that the Estate be given to the football club to build a new stadium while the grounds of the football club are used to house the remaining residents of the Estate. Eventually, after eighteen months, the St. Patrick's Athletic proposal is rejected.

1999: Dublin City Council purchases two sites adjacent to the Estate as part of an initial phase of regeneration. Construction begins on each of these sites and over the next two years 101 housing units are built on them. In the grounds of Goldenbridge Convent a mixture of houses and apartments are built, fifty-one in all, while at the Bulfin Road entrance to the Estate fifty housing units are built to accommodate older people from the Estate.

2001: The St. Michael's Estate Blocks' Committee establishes a Community Regeneration Team. The Team is made up of local residents and community and voluntary organisations working on and around the Estate. The idea behind the Team is to set up and develop an autonomous community 'think tank'. The Community Regeneration Team has met on a weekly basis from then right up to the present.

2001: Dublin City Council launches a new framework plan for the Estate. This plan is entitled 'Moving Ahead' and a period of three months is given over for consultation with residents of the Estate. Residents' core recommendation is that the plan contain houses with front and back gardens. A sub-group of the St. Michael's Estate Task Force is set up to oversee the development of this plan until it is lodged for planning permission. The design sub-group is made up of local residents, local community groups, City Councillors and staff from the City Council including an architect.

2002: *Past, Present and Future: A Community Vision for the Regeneration of St. Michael's Estate* is launched by the Blocks' Committee and the Community Regeneration Team. The document outlines what is important in regeneration from a community perspective and is used a benchmark document for the next number of years.

2002: Twenty two residents from St. Michael's Estate move into Bulfin Court as part of the first phase of regeneration.

2003: Fifty families from Blocks 1, 2, and 3 move into the newly constructed housing in Emmet Crescent which adjoins the Estate. A number of families also transfer off the Estate. The final detail of the 'Moving Ahead' plan is signed off by the design sub-group of the Task Force and is lodged with An Bord Pleannala (the Planning Board) for planning permission.

2003: The St. Michael's Estate Task Force is informed that the Department of the Environment has rejected the proposed 'Moving Ahead' master plan. The Department instead recommends that the Estate be regenerated using the mechanism of Public Private Partnership.

2004: Due to the anger and frustration at the rejection of the 'Moving Ahead' plan a campaign group is set up locally by the Community Regeneration Team. An official campaign is launched to reinstate the 'Moving Ahead' plan.
2004: Dublin City Council launches a completely new framework plan for the Estate. This plan is developed very much in isolation with no input from residents or community groups on the Estate. The plan also encompasses an extra three acre site at

the front of the Estate which adjoins Emmet Road. This new framework plan now contains 850 housing units and there is little proposed social housing on the plan. The plan is made up entirely of apartments with no conventional housing as demanded by the remaining residents.

2004: The Blocks vacated as part of the first phase are demolished. A large public meeting takes place in the local Parish Centre to discuss the City Council's new framework plan. At the end of the meeting the plan is rejected overwhelmingly by those present in the hall.

2004: A proposal is put to the chamber of Dublin City Council that the City Council's proposed new framework plan for St. Michael's Estate be rejected. All 52 City Councillors support the motion and the framework plan is officially rejected by the City Council Chamber.

2004: Dublin City Council re-enters negotiations with residents and other members of the Task Force to try to negotiate a settlement to the conflict over regeneration. This process is facilitated by the chairperson of the Task Force and, after protracted negotiations, basic agreements are reached on the tenure mix of the new estate, the proposed heights for the project and the community facilities and services to go on the new estate.

2005: The agreements reached as part of the negotiations form the basis for a 'brief' to be given out to interested developers. The formal PPP process begins with an advertisement being placed in the *Irish Times* newspaper. Initially there is a surge of interest, but eventually a small group of four development consortia retain an interest in the project. Each of these is given a detailed 'Request for Proposals' (RFP) outlining what is required for the new estate.

2005: The St. Michael's Estate Task Force is disbanded and a new structure, the St. Michael's Estate Regeneration Board is set up. The remit of the Regeneration Board is specifically to oversee the physical and social regeneration of the Estate. It has significantly more resources and powers than the preceding Task Force structure. The new Board is made up of local residents, community and voluntary groups, Dublin City Council, the Gardai and local City Councillors. The Board has a new independent chairperson and is allocated the resources to employ a full time Chief Executive Officer and an administrator. The Board is currently working to establish itself as a Limited Company.

2006: After more than a year of negotiating, a local resident and a member of the Community Regeneration Team participate on the 'Assessment Panel' whereby a developer is chosen from one of the four bidders. This is the first time that this has happened on any PPP project within the State.

January 2007: the Development Consortia, McNamara/ Castlethorn, is chosen as the 'Preferred Bidder' for the regeneration of St. Michael's Estate. Following the choosing of the Preferred Bidder, much of the rest of the time in 2007 is given over to working on outstanding issues that need to be resolved in the McNamara/Castlethorn plan.

February 2008: The 'Project Agreement', the contract governing the content of the new plans for the regeneration of St. Michael's Estate under PPP, is signed off by the St. Michael's Estate Regeneration Board. The plan goes to Dublin City Council for formal ratification.

May 2008 – After months of negotiations Dublin City Council announces that the Public Private Partnership which it had with McNamara/Castlethorn in St. Michael's Estate will not go ahead. (Four other PPP projects involving the City Council and McNamara Construction also collapse). Some months later McNamara/Castlethorn officially withdraw from the PPP in St. Michael's Estate.

Preface

The Right to Housing as a Right to Life

KATHLEEN LYNCH

The 'right to housing' is an integral element of the 'right to life': without a safe, secure and inviolable dwelling, not only is a person denied one of life's basic goods, she or he is denied access to the realisation of other rights, including the right to health, education, and privacy, and the right to found a family, and to engage effectively in economic, social and public life. The right to adequate housing is enshrined in many international legal instruments to which Ireland is party, including the Universal Declaration of Human Rights (Article 25) and the International Covenant on Economic, Social and Cultural Rights (ESCR) (Article 11). Moreover, the UN monitoring committee for the ESCR has spelt out what is meant by 'adequate housing': it includes having security of tenure, the availability of services and infrastructure, and housing which is affordable, habitable and accessible (Drudy and Punch, 2005: 183-4).

Given the size of the country, its considerable wealth and the relatively small population, there should be no shortage of housing, or of land for housing, in Ireland. Yet, there is, especially in our cities. That this shortage is an orchestrated one serving powerful commercial and political interests (because of the failure of successive governments to act to protect housing needs as recommended by the Kenny Report over 30 years ago) is well known. There is both ample space and resources to house everyone in Ireland if the political will was there to do it.

One major reason why housing needs have been neglected is because housing has not been treated as a basic human right requiring full State protection. Rather, housing has been defined as a 'commodity'; it has been equated with 'property' (exemplified in the proliferation of *Property Supplements* in all of the major newspapers and property-related programmes on television), an investment like any other, something those with excess wealth can 'invest in' and profit from, often with the assistance of the government, through a host of tax concessions. In contrast to the proliferation of property supplements, there are no Housing Supplements, and little attention is paid to those who cannot afford to buy a home of their own. Yet, a sizeable and growing minority of people in Ireland cannot afford to buy a home. Using national data, Drudy and Punch (ibid: 113) estimate that about 250,000 persons and 140,000 household were in housing need in 2005, and this did not take account of persons, such as disabled persons, who may be inappropriately housed.

This book is about those people who cannot afford to buy a home of their own and who live in public housing; it shows how their housing needs have been redefined and undermined in the new millennium as fewer and fewer publicly-owned houses are built. In particular, it tells the story of a working-class community's engagement with the representatives of the State in defending their rights to housing in an urban regeneration context.

The story that is told is profoundly disturbing because of the many inequalities it documents in the 'regeneration' process, including inequalities in power, resources and capacity between the State and its agents, and local communities. It explodes many myths about public-private 'partnerships', demonstrating in particular the deep lack of respect by the State for 'poor people on rich land' who are being 'regenerated'. While agents of the State did engage with the local community in St. Michael's Estate about their housing needs in planning their 'regeneration', when the community's needs and wishes did not synchronise with strategic political interests in freeing up publicly-owned land for 'development', the community's democratically expressed needs and interests were set aside.

The community did not accept their relegation to the periphery however; they fought back for the right to engage in designing and planning their own housing. So this book is not just about inequalities in wealth, power, status and influence as exemplified in the housing field, it is also about solidarity and hope. It is about the power and capabilities of people who are organised, and who use their democratic voice effectively to be heard and heeded within the corridors of power. It is a chronicle of hope as much as a record of class-related disrespect.

What is unique about the book is that it documents how the process of 'housing regeneration' works from the inside, from the perspective of those who are being 'regenerated'. It is written from the perspective of ordinary citizens, people who only became community activists by accident of history, when they had to defend their right to a home of their own. The insider perspective is provided through the systematically documented experiences of local residents during regeneration. It is a research dialogue between the author, residents and community workers, all of whom were party to the interpreting and editing of the work. It also records systematically the State's responses to the residents, including engagement, denials and dismissals.

The book is also a rich research resource. With the help of his co-workers and the residents in St. Michael's Estate in Dublin, Dr. John Bissett uses his considerable sociological expertise to critically analyse the process of regeneration from an egalitarian perspective. He documents and interprets the regeneration process, highlighting the power of commercial interests in Dublin city in determining the path of 'regeneration'. Using a critical analytic lens, the book systematically documents the way in which the State is beholden to profit-oriented financial interests, at the expense of poorer people in society. It shows, in a very raw form, where power lies in any 'partnership for regeneration' between agents of the state and low-income communities; it rests outside that dyad. Those who exercise most power do not attend partnership meetings about regeneration but they are present at such meetings through the influence they exercise, directly and indirectly, in the funding of urban development and re-development. The book is therefore both a rich source of scientific evidence on how the process of regeneration was negotiated and delivered over several years, and a critical social scientific analysis of that process informed by local resident's understanding. It shows the circuitous routes of power, at times direct and visible, and at other times indirect and invisible.

The book is not only of value as a scientific resource, it is also instructive methodologically in terms of what it tells us about doing research from the inside. It exemplifies the merits of transdisciplinary study, research that combines insider understanding of a research subject with academic expertise drawing on a range of disciplinary perspectives. It is a rare achievement in this regard.

Trailing the minutiae and micro politics of regeneration, the book also raises profound ethical and political questions for policy-makers and politicians. The voices of those with urgent housing needs are raised outside of their own community asking 'who is taking responsibility in Ireland for protecting the right to housing as a basic human right?'

PROFESSOR KATHLEEN LYNCH is Chair of Equality Studies at UCD where she holds a Senior Lectureship in Education. She is the founder of the UCD Equality Studies Centre, established in 1990, and founder of the UCD School of Social Justice, established in 2005. She serves in a voluntary capacity on a number of boards for statutory, community and voluntary agencies.

Chapter 1

The Grassroots and Regeneration

When everyone is equal there is no politics, for politics involves subordinates and superiors.[3]

The first man who, having enclosed a piece of ground, bethought himself of saying 'This is mine,' and found people simple enough to believe him, was the real founder of civil society. From how many crimes, wars, and murders, from how many horrors and misfortunes might not have anyone saved mankind, by pulling up the stakes, or filling up the ditch, and crying to his fellows: 'Beware of listening to this impostor; you are undone if you once forget that the fruits of the earth belong to us all, and the earth itself to nobody'.[4]

INTRODUCTION

In an ideal world urban regeneration would be based on mutual agreement and consensus. All of the respective parties would sit round and work out, through dialogue, the redefining of an estate for the future. The various perspectives and views would intermingle producing a truly collaborative vision. There would be equality between all participants to the process, reflected in a symmetrical balance of influence. Every party would participate in the debate from the same basis and on the same conditions. All proposals and changes would be based on common agreement. Power and domination would be absent from the debate.

Equality would permeate all aspects of the work. The spirit of the endeavour would be one of cooperation and collaboration, mutual respect and appreciation. The project would have a democratic, ethical core and would be about meeting the needs of people, especially those in greatest need.

This book is a community-based account of the regeneration of St. Michael's Estate. St. Michael's Estate was, for over thirty five years, a working class, publicly-owned housing estate on the fringes of Dublin's inner city. Over a period of years the Estate became something of a pariah, set adrift from the rest of Inchicore and the city in general. The physical and material conditions on the Estate reflected sustained and endemic deprivation. Multiple inequalities cross referenced each other and to a great extent provided the impetus and desire for regeneration in the first place. In 1998, tenants and residents agreed as part of a formal survey to have the Estate totally demolished and a new estate built in its place. They hoped that lives would be transformed and things would be better than before. Little could they have imagined what was to follow. This book attempts to understand the unexpected realities of regeneration by painting a picture of the community of St. Michael's Estate in recent years. It is an exploration of a community's engagement and struggle with regeneration and pays particular attention to the maintenance and sustaining of patterns of inequality and relations of power. The book argues that as the process unfolded, inequality became a significant and enduring characteristic across the political, economic and social terrain of regeneration.

The attempt to shape the future definition of St. Michael's Estate has taken place between a number of parties. They include the Irish State (both local and central), local tenants and residents, local community organisations and groups (working with residents), local political representatives, and private developers. Unpacking the nature and structure of the relationships between the various parties is critical to understanding regeneration overall. One of the core contentions of this work is that hierarchies of power clearly exist and are maintained within such sets of relations. Not only do these hierarchies exist, but they also have a direct bearing on the objectives and outcomes of regeneration. A fundamental question that has emerged over the course of this process is, who is regeneration for? In other words, what should such a project strive to do and for whom? In the case of St Michael's Estate, there were clearly different visions and interpretations from the respective groups and parties, and the clearest to emerge were those between community-based visions of regeneration and those of the State.

The relationship between the State and local residents and community organisations was the pivotal relationship of the entire process. This relationship has gone through many phases but the experience has been characterised more by struggle, conflict and difference than by dialogue or consensus. Part of the reason for this undoubtedly has to do with the State's refusal to countenance any mode of regeneration other than that of Public Private Partnership. The experience of regeneration in St. Michael's Estate would suggest that the actions of the State have done more to maintain and consolidate inequalities of power than they did to change them.

IT HAS TO BE PUBLIC PRIVATE PARTNERSHIP

In August 2003, the Department of the Environment recommended that St. Michael's Estate be regenerated using the mechanism of Public Private Partnership (PPP)[5]. Such a framework was completely new to residents and community organisations on the Estate. Prior to this both the City Council and the community had spent two years developing a detailed publicly-funded masterplan for the Estate. The plan was the culmination of a number of years' work which had been initiated in 1998 when residents had 'identified their preferred option for the future of St. Michael's Estate as the demolition of the present structure and its replacement by a Dublin Corporation owned housing scheme'.[6] This changeover to PPP was to have a significant and dramatic effect on the entire process. All of the plans that had been developed were effectively scrapped and everyone had to start again from scratch. From the State's perspective there simply was no other way. It was PPP or nothing. Residents especially came to understand that the changing policies of the State would play a crucial role in the redefinition of the Estate and consequently their futures. The use and effects of state power are core themes of regeneration. Based on local experience, this power was experienced more as a disciplinary 'power over' than a collaborative 'power to'. It was local residents and community organisations that challenged such power.

One of the recurrent manifestations of State power came in the form of legitimate authority. Whether it was a letter from a State department or an official sitting at a meeting such authority was used to achieve or to further the State's objectives. The logic behind such authority was that the State alone had the expertise for projects of this scale. Ultimately, the State retained a veto over the regeneration process. In St. Michael's Estate, State power operated not only at a macro level with the changeover to PPP, but also in the daily grind of regeneration. Gaining and keeping control over the fine detail of PPP required ongoing monitoring, supervision and perseverance by State officials and departments.

At the heart of the regeneration has been the issue of the ownership, control and use of the land of St. Michael's Estate. As landlord and guardian the State would, at a critical moment in 2003, exercise its property rights over the Estate. Residents may have had an informal possession of the land by way of their living there but within PPP, social housing[7] tenancies were to be drastically reduced. PPP was used as an attempt to reclaim the land by the City Council and to use it in other ways. The relationship between landlord and tenant underwent a dramatic reorientation so that although the twenty first century is a different era, it has echoes of a feudal mode of relations. Given the exponential increase in property values and its location close to the city centre, the land of the Estate became phenomenally valuable. St. Michael's Estate was a 'Celtic Tiger' regeneration. Within such a context many questions arose including how the land would be used and to what ends? Who would benefit? Would a new social housing complex be built there to replace the existing one? What control would residents have over the future of the land? The land of the Estate became the prism through which the power of the State revealed itself. But it did not do so solely on its own terms, uncontested.

THE GRASSROOTS AND REGENERATION

In contrast to the stereotypical images in the media and the public sphere, there is a rich history in St. Michael's Estate. In particular, there has been a deep-rooted and radical seam of grassroots community work and local organisation on the Estate for over twenty years. Like residents themselves, such histories and traditions are often marginalised and silenced. However, the embeddedness of this grassroots work was to have a key impact on the overall regeneration process. It was from such a foundation that a counter-energy, prioritising residents' needs and community-based objectives, emerged. The articulation of this community perspective and the arguing for it became an unexpected theme of the entire regeneration process. This articulation took many forms and shapes and constituted a potent form of community power and influence. At its core were the ideas that both the process and outcomes of regeneration should be democratic and egalitarian. There was an awareness locally, given the State's objectives, that this would be a difficult and daunting endeavour. In fact, the entire structuring of regeneration, in particular the maintenance of dominant-subordinate relationships underwent, and continues to undergo, vociferous challenge.

Local organisation and community work have been part of the landscape in St. Michael's Estate for many years. But the sheer scale of regeneration was to pose new problems and challenges. The process would place an onerous weight on local tenants and organisations. Regeneration was a multi-faceted phenomenon which involved the navigation of a range of diverse fields and disciplines. Even without the overt politics of PPP, it included the intricacies of urban planning and design, architecture, housing policy and politics, general economics, community work itself, and somewhat unexpectedly, communications. Given such diversity, a question arose as to how a community could respond and organise itself? How would residents of the Estate define what was important to them? The bringing together of a 'Community Regeneration Team', was a critical organisational act in this respect. The impetus for this came from the local tenants' association, the St. Michael's Estate Blocks' Committee and the local community development project, the Family Resource Centre. The Community Regeneration Team was largely built on existing community infrastructure and provided a space for reflection and action based on local needs. The Team attempted to develop a praxis of sorts where thinking and action on regeneration were fused.

An early action, which developed through dialogue with the Blocks' Committee, was the production of a community-based vision for regeneration. It was a statement that a community was 'for' something and not just reacting to imposed ideas. *Past, Present and Future: A Community Vision for the Regeneration of St. Michael's Estate,*[8] was a simple but powerful encapsulation of what was important in regeneration from a community perspective. It was especially clear that the process should be primarily for social housing tenants and should attempt to tackle head on the prevalent social issues on the Estate. This document was written in what was ostensibly a co-operative phase of the regeneration prior to PPP. The changeover to PPP effectively ruptured such a collaboration. Within this changed structural context for regeneration, the struggle for equality and democracy became more pronounced. With PPP, regeneration became intensely politicised and spilled over into the general public sphere. The changed context provoked an intense and sustained debate both within and without the Estate. The process that ensued is the subject of this book.

A NOTE ON METHOD

I am a community worker with the Canal Communities Local Drugs Task Force (CCLDTF).[9] My main job is to support community representatives from the Canal Communities Area (Rialto, Inchicore, Bluebell) on the CCLDTF. It was through this work that my involvement with the regeneration of St. Michael's Estate began. In February 2001, I was invited to become a participant on the Community Regeneration Team. I accepted the invitation and have been a member of the Team from then right through to the present. From the outset the Team was made up of community workers, residents and local activists and has worked very much from a community work/development model since its inception. In September 2003, I proposed to my colleagues on the Regeneration Team that I would try and do some basic qualitative research into understanding what was happening on the Estate under the broad heading of 'urban regeneration'. There are few documented accounts of urban regeneration in Ireland from such an insider perspective. At the outset, the aim was merely to provide a general understanding of the process which was informed by broad questions such as 'How does a community such as St. Michael's Estate participate in its own regeneration?' I was following the 'what is it', 'what's happening here' and 'how is it done' sorts of questions. In this early phase, I was very much interested in a community's approach to the entire regeneration process. Within weeks of beginning this work, however, the entire regeneration process was turned upside down with the recommendation from the Department of the Environment to use Public Private Partnership as the mechanism for regeneration. This change was to have a profound effect on both the process and outcomes of regeneration. The mechanism reflected the changing values of the State and became hugely determinant in charting a new course for the regeneration of the Estate. PPP would become the master narrative for regeneration and would critically affect the entire process down to its most minute detail.

I have used the research technique of participant observation to record the regeneration process in St. Michael's Estate. Given the nature of regeneration, this methodology proved extremely appropriate to the job at hand. Whenever possible, I took notes and wrote up a regeneration journal. I followed the regeneration process into whatever spaces I could and attempted to record as much as possible and make some early attempts at comprehension. The timeframe for this covers the period from September 2003 until late 2007. The data used in this book is based primarily on recorded observations in recent years in St. Michael's Estate. At various junctures I have analysed these notes looking for significant themes and patterns that were emerging. I have also given a number of presentations to the Regeneration Team in St. Michael's Estate and to staff and students in the Equality Studies Centre, School of Social Justice, University College Dublin. These sessions have acted not only as a way of informing the group as to the nature of the research, but also of exploring ideas and themes that were emerging from the work. This work attempts to reflect the changing nature of regeneration and to capture in some small way, something of a community's intense struggle with regeneration through PPP. More recently, and right up until publication, all members of the Regeneration Team as well as a group of people who have no involvement have been reading and critiquing drafts of this work.

To conclude and reiterate then, this book deconstructs the nature and form of 'regeneration' as it took place in St. Michael's Estate in recent years. What can we learn from the process? How does it work, what are its objectives and who is it for? I argue here that PPP is a 'market-driven' mode of regeneration which is structured and conditioned by the necessities and values of the commercial housing market. Within PPP, the needs of the market came to dominate the process with the attempt to minimise the social and public aspects of the project. One of my key concerns, therefore, is with understanding and articulating patterns of inequality both in the imposition and the doing of PPP. A second aim, arising from the actual process in St. Michael's Estate, is to describe how grassroots challenges to the market-driven model emerged and to assess their significance, in particular, the development and articulation of an alternative model of regeneration, based on the values of equality, democracy, social justice and sustainability.

The book is structured in the following way. Chapter 2 gives an overview of the changing policy context of urban regeneration in Dublin in recent decades. Chapter 3 traces the social history of the Estate from its construction in 1969-1970 right up until its present phase of demolition. In Chapter 4, there is an outline of the history of community work on the Estate beginning in the mid-1980s. Chapter 5 begins the story of the current phase of regeneration proper, the State's decision not to go ahead with an agreed publicly-funded masterplan and its decision to change over to the mechanism of PPP. Chapter 6 looks at how the community of St. Michael's Estate responded to such a rejection and its struggle to fight its way back into the regeneration process. Chapter 7 takes the reader through the 'realpolitik' of regeneration. These were the hard-edged negotiations which took place in relation to the numbers of social, affordable and private housing that would make up the new estate as well as community and commercial facilities. Over the past three to four years, St. Michael's Estate was part of a citywide process, connecting in with other Dublin communities who were and are facing similar changes. This citywide process is covered in Chapter 8 of the book. The technical detail of working one's way through PPP and the difficulties any community faces, not least in understanding the process, are the subject of Chapter 9. The concluding part of the book in Chapter 10 attempts to 'deconstruct regeneration' and to find out what its really all about.

Chapter 2

The Regeneration Game:

Reshaping the City

Cities are in a constant state of formation, and nowhere is that more apparent than in Dublin at the turn of the twenty first century. Building and rebuilding activities dissolve and recreate different areas as sites of activity and use. Whether it is the refurbishment of City Hall or the development of a public plaza at Smithfield, the road works necessitated by the building of Luas or the reinvention of the Guinness Plant as a state-of-the art digital media hub, Dubliners have become accustomed to living in a city that is somewhat chaotically in the making. [10]

In order to understand what is happening in St. Michael's Estate we need to place it in a wider context of recent social and urban change in Irish society generally and in Dublin more specifically. Socially, St. Michael's Estate had become a pariah estate set adrift from the rest of the Inchicore community and the city in general, but it still remained caught up in a set of critical relationships, especially those with the State. The most obvious of these changing institutional relationships was the rent-based, landlord-tenant relationship between tenants and Dublin City Council. Over the intervening years, the nature and scope of this relationship would fundamentally alter. In hindsight, residents' straightforward view that it was a local, *quid pro quo* situation of trading flats for houses with front and back gardens, did not take account of the evolving policy context of urban regeneration in the city. St. Michael's was about to embark on a journey that other communities and neighbourhoods in the city had previously experienced. The rules of engagement for the regeneration game were being written and modified from a distance. The Irish State had been travelling its own regeneration journey since 1986 and was developing clear ideas as to its expectations and objectives from regeneration in general. The people of St. Michael's Estate had little knowledge of this changing context.

Key issues, pervasive in regeneration at this broader structural level, included the control and definition of the objectives of regeneration, the form and shape of regeneration structures and governance bodies, and the implementation and effects of broader state policies of finance and planning, for example, the use of public private partnerships and the new housing philosophy of 'social mix'. St. Michael's Estate found itself thrust into the centre of this changing ideological context, the implications of which took some time to become clear. The ideas and practices that were changing the physical fabric of the city were themselves undergoing something of a metamorphosis. Since 1986, urban regeneration has evolved and taken on new shapes and forms in response to critique and the conditions and circumstances of the time. The import of this is that there isn't a single, overarching regeneration model that has been universally applied. The models are many and varied. Outlining the contours of these changes will help us to place the Estate within this broader regeneration field.

URBAN REGENERATION AND THE 'ENTREPRENEURIAL' CITY

Ireland's socio-economic history in the twentieth century saw it successively change the basis of its mode of development within a relatively short space of time.[11] From being a pre-industrial society in the early twentieth century, Ireland went through a brief period of industrialisation and is now considered by some to be a post-industrial society.[12] Urban regeneration in Ireland has therefore taken place within the changed context of the developing 'tiger' economy, and the modernisation of Irish society.[13] It is perhaps no coincidence that the two are almost identical chronological processes. Given its position as the capital city, with over one-third of the Irish population resident there, Dublin has been the site of the most prolific urban change in recent decades. Urban planning underwent a distinct reorientation in Dublin in the mid-1980s, with the city attempting to reposition itself, like many others, within a newly emerging global context.[14] Until then, the inner city had been left to decay and the suburbanisation of the city had been the pivotal planning dynamic for over twenty years. The 'Myles Wright' planning strategy,[15] adopted in the 1960s, saw a number of new towns built on the periphery of Dublin including Blanchardstown, Clondalkin/Lucan, Tallaght and Ballymun. The city centre was neglected and virtually undeveloped during this period. St. Michael's Estate was one of the last, if not the last, social housing flat complex to be built in the city in 1969-70.

In the mid-1980s there was a sharp reaction against Dublin becoming an American 'doughnut' type city with a hollowed out centre and a bloated periphery. Partly in response to critiques of the strategy of suburbanisation and to a changing political-economic context, urban planning underwent a profound reorientation. The Urban Renewal and Finance Acts of 1986 provided a legislative framework within which this new model of urban regeneration would take place. Specific areas of the city were designated for renewal and developers were further encouraged through the provision of significant tax incentives for development. Two State departments co-ordinated the policy change, the Department of Finance and the Department of the Environment. It was within this period that "Dublin governance took on the institutional dimensions of the 'entrepreneurial' city".[16] The reins of this process were held tightly by a newly-elected central government. Changes in the bodypolitic in the form of a new coalition government were bringing about changes in the urban policy of the city. The redevelopment of the city would be based on a new set of strategies much of which revolved around attracting investment and giving the city an international profile. An appropriate legislative framework, setting up controlling corporations and the designation of specific areas as regeneration ready, were all central to these strategies. The power over this process at this early stage remained highly centralised within the State.

FLAGSHIP PROJECTS: THE CUSTOM HOUSE DOCKS AND TEMPLE BAR

The flagship project chosen to kick-start the new policy was the Custom House Docks site in Dublin's north east inner city in 1986. An Urban Development Corporation (UDC) known as the Custom House Docks Development Association (CHDDA) was set up to oversee this development and was given special powers of planning. In retrospect this scheme, which had at its heart the development of the Irish Financial Services Centre, was something of the original of the species and has been characterised as "the first effective model of urban regeneration in Ireland".[17] The CHDDA was modelled on the Urban Development Corporations that had been pioneered in Britain and was initiated by central government while Dublin Corporation, as Dublin City Council was then known, was all but excluded from the project.[18] Upon evaluation, the Custom House Docks regeneration project was criticised for its explicit focus on physical and economic regeneration.[19] There was no real attempt to integrate the project with the surrounding communities in the north inner city nor was there any real thought given to the social implications of regeneration:

> ...the mono-functional landscape of the UDP site has isolated it from surrounding communities and from Dublin City as a

whole. This isolation is reinforced by the presence of security guards and by the perpetual monitoring of the area through CCTV. Electronic security gates, a moat, a wall several metres in height (referred to by the local communities as the 'Berlin Wall') segregate the indigenous communities from the 'new' communities established after the CHDA regeneration.[20]

The Custom House Docks approach to urban regeneration resonates and has many parallels with the fortified 'city of quartz' that Davis[21] has described coming into being in Los Angeles. Paradoxically, the Custom House Docks regeneration project intensified social polarisation. The changes led to a professional-isation and gentrification of the area and large-scale restructuring of a community along social class lines. The CHDDA was forbidden by law from providing social housing on the site. In existing local communities unemployment also rose during the period of the development. One of the consequences was to substantially increase the value of property which in turn led to an overall reduction in the availability of social and affordable housing in the north east inner city area. Future generations of urban villagers who lived in the area were priced out of the local housing market. In the late 1990s, the CHDDA was restructured and became the Dublin Docklands Development Authority (DDDA). This new authority attempted to redress the explicit shortcomings of the earlier model. The overtly exclusive nature of the original authority had forced a rethink in strategy. Much of the energy and resistance to the authoritarian model came from grassroots organisations and community activists working in the north-east inner city. [22]

An attempt to redress the impenetrability of the Custom House Docks development came with the regeneration of Temple Bar on the south side of the River Liffey in 1991. Because of the worldwide economic downturn at the end of the 1980s, the regeneration of Temple Bar had a qualitatively differ-ent focus than the Custom House Docks. This project revolved not around attracting large corporations into gleaming new office towers and providing gated spaces for them, but around the themes of culture, heritage and tourism and returning people to the city. The objective of regeneration had changed slightly, "the Temple Bar Plan proposed a 'people oriented' site with a permeable urban fabric and high quality open spaces".[23] Powers of planning over the development were returned to Dublin City Council, and it was given a stronger monitoring role over the process. The City Council had a partnership role and developed a joint framework architectural plan with Temple Bar Properties, the overall manager and private partner in the project. The reinstatement of local government in the planning process was an attempt to redress the acute imbalance which had existed in the Custom House Docks between central and local government. The regeneration of Temple Bar, however, was still principally private sector driven and did little to change the corporate model that had existed in the Custom House Docks. Perhaps the most significant change was Dublin City Council's resurrection as a limited participant in the regeneration process. The reintroduction of local government is perhaps the defining characteristic of this second model of regeneration. The control of regeneration had shifted slightly and the City Council would continue to reposition itself and adapt organisationally in order to find a niche for itself within a rapidly changing city. One of these adaptation strategies involved establishing a development team with robust corporate values within the City Council itself. The property development section of Dublin City Council, the *Inner City Development Team* (ICDT) had a great deal of flexibility in responding to developers and consortia in relation to development in the city.

Both the Custom House Docks and Temple Bar schemes were primarily characterised by a direct relationship between the central State and development companies. This relationship was mediated through urban development corporations. Perhaps the most striking characteristic of both of these approaches to urban regeneration was their anti-democratic and exclusive nature. The distribution of power in these early projects remained within tightly-controlled and monitored networks. There was a clear perception from within the State that local government was too bureaucratic and too inflexible to have any major role within such programmes. Consideration of, or involvement with communities, was not part of those schemes. However, with the publication of a critical evaluation of the Custom House Docks and Temple Bar regeneration programmes[24] in 1996, the ground began to shift. The evaluation had been commissioned by the Department of the Environment to assess "the impact, effectiveness and cost of the Urban Renewal Schemes".[25] In the face of mounting criticism from various quarters, central government began exploring the possibilities for a new approach. This new approach has been described as an 'adaptive entrepreneurial' model. The property-led models that had dominated Temple Bar and the Custom House Docks would be softened with a more holistic, comprehensive approach to urban regeneration. Regeneration was to be multi-layered and would include social and cultural dimensions which went beyond the purely economic/physical.

Within this new approach, the City Council would reclaim a role for itself within 'micro-area' planning in specific sections of the city. Communities would also be given a more substantial role in the process. If the content was to change, then the models must reflect this through the increased participation of those sectors who had been all but excluded. This necessitated trying to develop new structural models for regeneration which were more partic-ipative and democratic than either the Custom House Docks or Temple Bar. Local government, residents and community-based organisations needed to be brought fully into the process. This shift in emphasis and orientation has been described in positive terms by Bartley and Treadwell Shine in their analysis of the changing dynamics of urban regeneration in Dublin:

> The initial concern with securing property led economic objec-tives through a technocratic style of management has given way to approaches based upon broad partnership schemes that seek to achieve a wider mix of economic and social objectives for targeted areas. [26]

HISTORIC AREA REJUVENATION PROJECT (HARP)

The search for a more holistic form of urban regeneration under-pinned by more democratic forms of governance began with the Historic Area Rejuvenation Project (HARP) project in the Markets/Smithfield area in Dublin's northwest inner city. The organisation and objectives of regeneration underwent some-thing of a transformation. The introduction of the HARP model signalled a toning down of the corporate model that had existed previously. Local government had been re-established in a pivotal leadership role in urban regeneration. The HARP model offered the possibility of accommodating a diverse range of interests across a variety of sectors and on the surface encapsulated a pluralistic participative methodology. The HARP approach allowed for considerable involvement by local community repre-sentatives "... in this model the local authority leads the potential public-private sector partnerships but the community and other elements of 'civil society' are actively drawn into the partner-ship".[27] The HARP project moved, mirroring national structures, toward a partnership between community, state and private sectors. One of the signal changes was the reintroduction of local government as an enabling authority into a key co-ordinating role with urban regeneration. For the first time, the community sector had a clearly identified structural role within urban regen-eration. In practical terms, this meant the collaborative drawing up of a local area action plan for the HARP area. The HARP model was an attempt at democratising the earlier versions of urban regeneration. It was also the forerunner to the introduction of the current and most recent regeneration model initiated by the City Council.

INTEGRATED AREA PLANS

Integrated Area Plans (IAP) are the most recent model of urban regeneration to be introduced by the State. The IAP mechanism was established to respond to a variety of needs including social, cultural, employment and educational as well as the more obvious one of physical reconstruction. A number of areas[28] were designated for IAPs and invited to draw up strategic local action plans covering a broad range of issues for their areas. In line with the changing perspective on urban regeneration these local area plans were to cover much more than economic terrain:

> IAPs are localised planning mechanisms which aim to embrace the complexity of contemporary urban systems through developing a holistic approach toward the achievement of social, economic and environmental goals while encouraging the necessary inter-sectoral co-ordination to achieve such aims. [29]

The Integrated Area Plan approach was introduced toward the end of the 1990s and became a key component of the City Development Plan in 1999. The approach was used in a number of designated areas of Dublin City. The evolution of this area specific regeneration perspective emerges from the objectives of the programme, chief among which was to 'achieve sustainable urban regeneration through a framework of interventions that achieves a balance of social, physical and economic renewal'.[30] The IAP process would do this by attracting mainly private investment into the designated areas in order to deliver a broad range of infrastructure ranging from roads and housing to community and commercial facilities. The IAPs would also create mechanisms and frameworks to ensure that the social dimension of urban renewal extends tangible benefits to local residents. The IAP process has been in place since 1998 and continues to operate in defined areas at the time of writing.

ASSESSING AN IAP: THE LIBERTIES/COOMBE

In retrospect, one could be forgiven for assuming that 'regeneration' has gone through a positive evolutionary process and is inexorably and inevitably becoming more inclusive and democratic. However, serious questions have been raised for some time about the grounds for such confidence and optimism. There are critical distributory questions as to the benefits of regeneration. A second set of questions are process related and ask how is regeneration being done? It seems that we have arrived at another much needed stage of critical review. The evaluation of the property-led urban regeneration projects in the Custom House Docks and Temple Bar led to a change in approach, but the new IAP approach it engendered, is now itself facing a growing critique. One of the strongest of these critiques has come from a community that entered into the process genuinely but found the experience to be far from the original rhetoric:

> In essence, the community understood the *Liberties/Coombe Integrated Area Plan* to be an invitation to the community to leave the confrontational nature of past exchanges between the community and statutory sector behind. It understood it to be an invitation to enter – as an equal partner – into a clearly delineated and structured process which would bring about the sustainable urban regeneration of the south west inner city by integrating physical, social and economic objectives. [31]

Significant events occurred which effectively precluded this relationship of equality from coming into being. The original role envisaged for the overseeing group of the IAP was changed mid-stream from a powerful steering role, to a much weakened monitoring role over the process. Fundamental controls over the process were vested elsewhere, principally with An Bord Pleannala (the Planning Board) and, perhaps less visibly with developers. The Liberties Coombe IAP highlighted the nature of power and powerlessness in urban regeneration. Power operated in a number of ways. The community was excluded from access to meaningful resources to participate and community knowledge took on more and more of a subordinate position within the overall IAP process. Power also operated through the language and discourse of planning which functioned insidiously as a mechanism of exclusion and marginalisation. Regeneration became a struggle where "Community representatives were confronted at every turn by a whole relationship of power and inequality vested in the technical language and professional jargon".[32] From a position of apparent equality at the outset, the community sector experienced a fate whereby its stake in the implementation of the Liberties Coombe IAP was diminishing before its eyes. The community experience of the Liberties Coombe IAP was demoralising for those who participated. The outcomes in the IAP process favoured developers and were facilitated by the City Council and An Bord Pleannala. The experience has left the community angry and deeply sceptical of the entire IAP process:

> When this inner city community surveys the landscape of the Liberties, it can now see with great clarity what the net outcome of the Liberties/Coombe Integrated Area Plan and its centrepiece – the Cork Street Coombe Bypass - has been: ... ever increasing building heights and densities in wildly inappropriate and overblown private gated apartments...the displacement of the resident community which will always follow as an inevitable consequence of the influx of private capital as land and property values rise; the auction and privatisation of publicly held lands at a time when the shortage of publicly owned land is being cited as one of the major barriers to the provision of social housing; the failure to secure any social housing units from the extensive private residential development taking place in the area. [33]

The community perspective on the Liberties IAP poses profound questions as to the nature of this type of urban regeneration. The IAP model promised great things, not least a democratisation of regeneration structures and, it was hoped, positive outcomes. It appears that in the Liberties Coombe area of Dublin's inner city, the search for a multi-layered, holistic regeneration along social, cultural and economic lines went unfulfilled. The new model also had some old problems. Even the participatory structures which were put in place were quickly watered down and had their powers diminished and reduced shortly after their inception. At its core, asymmetrical relationships of power were sustained in this IAP and the interests of the powerful were given precedence.

The Cork Street/Coombe IAP covered an extensive area of inner city Dublin. But more recently, Dublin City Council has been sharpening the focus of its regeneration programme by targeting specific City Council flat complexes and estates and treating them as tightly contained developmental entities in and of themselves. St. Michael's Estate is one such complex. It lies within the Inchicore/Kilmainham IAP catchment area but the regeneration programme in recent years has been based on a direct relationship between the Estate and the City Council. To a great extent the regeneration of St. Michael's Estate has taken place outside of the Inchicore/Kilmainham IAP mechanism. This intensely focussed, estate-based approach to regeneration is part of a broader strategy targeting a number of estates across the city.

It may sound paradoxical, but the approach is both intensive and extensive at the same time. The approach is intensive in the sense that the City Council is dedicating project teams and resources to draw up detailed plans for each specific complex and estate. Within each estate, there is a high degree of hands-on work, close supervision and monitoring. And yet the strategy is extensive in the sense that each complex is part of a broader plan involving a large number of complexes and estates across the city. The scale of the change is therefore exponential, multiplying out from each individual complex to form part of a more general social process across the city. Along with St. Michael's Estate, a number of older complexes in the city including Fatima Mansions, O'Devaney Gardens, Dominic Street, St. Teresa's Gardens are all being worked with in this way. It would be misleading however to describe this process as completely state driven. Change in many of these complexes has been demanded for many years by tenants and community organisations. In recent years, the energy generated from within communities has been growing and there is much to suggest that communities are beginning to engage and to grapple with this change and to work out what's best for them.

SUMMARY

In this chapter we have delved into the changing nature of urban regeneration in Dublin over the past two decades. The approaches taken by the State have been varied to say the least. Currently many specific complexes and estates in the city have become micro-regeneration zones in and of themselves. The role of the City Council has also changed in recent years. Within the Custom House Docks model it was central government which was to the fore, and yet in recent years the City Council has regained a foothold in regeneration most obviously within the many local authority complexes in the city. The mechanism of Public Private Partnership has also emerged as the newly dominant mode of regeneration in many City Council estates. Having reviewed the recent history of regeneration in Dublin from this broad perspective we need to ask ourselves why is it that communities need to be regenerated in the first place? With this question in mind it is to the history of St. Michael's Estate that we now turn.

Chapter 3

The Making and Breaking of St. Michael's Estate

The blocks of flats on the land of St. Michael's Estate appear as if they were arbitrarily scattered like bird feed from a hand and stood where they came to rest. Each like a dice with its number up, landing somewhere on a board, like a chain of islands that just are, without logic. Each block peering toward its nearest neighbour knowing that without an earthquake, there will always be an unbridgeable chasm between them in this open hinterland. This place has been defined as much by the absolute spaces between buildings as it has by the buildings themselves. Each block out on its own as it were, living a very public life. Every side of every block lies exposed elementally and visually. There is little one can conceal. Out in the open, amidst the elements, something of St Michael's Estate always feels, like Prometheus, a little vulnerable to what might come along. As a housing estate it lacks the architectural intimacy of its neighbours in the rest of Inchicore. And yet the blocks stand dogged and resolute in the face of the elements.

(The Author)

S t. Michael's Estate is a Dublin City Council flat complex, which lies just over two miles from Dublin City Centre. It was built between 1969 and 1970 for families living on the existing site and also for new families moving from the inner city.

The site stands very close to the heart of the village of Inchicore to the west of Dublin city centre. To get to Inchicore one leaves the centre of the city and travels out, beyond the Pale, through the medieval Dublin of Christchurch, Thomas Street, James' Street and Kilmainham before climbing the hill on Emmet Road and arriving in one of the city's oldest urban villages. The land on which the Estate stands originally housed Richmond Barracks. The barracks was built by the British army for billeting troops prior to Irish independence. The area is a significant historical and heritage site. The only remaining barracks building (adjacent to the Estate and until very recently used as a Christian Brothers primary school) was used to detain many of the leaders of the 1916 rising prior to their removal to Kilmainham gaol for execution. After independence and British withdrawal the barracks was transformed into a series of tenements and utilised for public housing and was renamed firstly as Keogh Barracks and later as Keogh Square. Over time, the conditions on 'The Square' deteriorated giving rise to an impetus for change and at the end of the 1960s, a new estate materialised:

> Keogh Square, for a long time a city slum black spot, is to be the site of an ultra-modern scheme of centrally heated flat blocks which will cost more than £1,220,000. The Corporation's Housing Committee was told last night that in all 304 flats would be contained in blocks five to eight storeys high which would take about 70 weeks to build. It is expected that work will start early in the new year (*Evening Press*, 12 December, 1968).

After the razing of Keogh Square, fourteen blocks of flats were built on the site in a mixture of two, four, and eight storey structures. When finished in 1970, three hundred and forty six housing units were constructed. The estate is bordered on all sides. To the north is Emmet road and Inchicore village. To the south a historic city graveyard, the Grand Canal and the new LUAS red line. To the west is Vincent Street, Tyrone Place a smaller City Council flat complex, and the recently converted

Goldenbridge Convent. To the east is St. Michael's Christian Brothers' Primary School which officially closed in 2007. The Estate stands on 11 acres of land and was built using the same Balency construction system[34] used in the much larger complex in Ballymun, and when completed, resembled a miniature sibling of the much larger northside estate.

Architecturally, St. Michael's Estate was to make a distinct physical and social impression. The blocks were constructed from white pre-cast panels and each had a distinct black cap. Given that Dublin had a low-rise skyline for most of this period the blocks were visible from many parts of the city and acted as both landmark and reference point. The complex had a gritty, modernist feel to it physically. Nothing in its surroundings or anywhere in the metropolitan city compared to it. It was out of kilter with the Inchicore landscape. The design was much more in keeping with the suburban banlieus of Paris and Madrid than anything in the city. Not only was it a housing scheme it was also an architectural statement of change. It was a new and experimental urban form, a new way of living in the city. The heating system was concealed under floor with no plumbing paraphernalia anywhere to be seen. Living here was meant to give residents the best of both worlds, absolute internal privacy coupled with an unfettered access to an open plan landscape in the exterior. Such a coupling of interior and exterior was designed to accommodate the contrasting needs of the human psyche. Private and public consciousness could happily coexist, in theory at least. Another factor, perhaps the critical one, which undoubtedly influenced the design and construction of St. Michael's Estate, was that of cost. The building of some 346 flats in the configurations in which they were constructed had a direct relationship to cost. Land was not the ravenously scarce commodity that it is today. Building multiple housing units on top of each other using the most basic materials was not only a new architectural statement it was also cheap. The simple modernist aesthetics of the Estate were determined to a great extent by the economics of the time.

There is no comparable architectural complex in the metropolitan area of the city. It is also the only public housing complex of its generation in the metropolitan area of the city to use lifts, in the eight storey blocks. Most of the older complexes in the city, Fatima Mansions, Oliver Bond, Hardwicke Street, St. Joseph's Mansions, were designed with shared exterior balconies that opened out on to a common courtyard area. When residents ascended the stairs and walked on to the balconies of these older complexes they could still maintain verbal and visual contact with people in the block as they opened their doors. Hence the growth of the 'balcony culture' of inner city Dublin flat complexes. The blocks here, by contrast, were built around a central stairwell and the landings for accessing the flats were completely internal to the blocks. Unusually, each flat in St. Michael's Estate had its own individual, private balcony.

In retrospect, the demolition of Keogh Square and the origins of the 'ultra-modern' St. Michael's Estate are laden with an uncanny sense of *déjà vu*. The story of one local woman in a national newspaper evokes a sense of another time and place, and yet there is also a strong reverberation with the present:

> She wandered sadly through the ruins. For 43 years this was her home, 'and in my heart its still my home' she sighed. Mrs. Isabella McMahon of Rossmore Avenue Ballyfermot, was back at Keogh Square visiting old friends who were still waiting to be rehoused. The Square, one of the biggest blots on the Dublin housing landscape will shortly be no more. Most people would say 'good riddance' but for the old inhabitants it has many memories. They can recall happy times there, and it was clear from Ms McMahon that no matter how humble there's no place like home. With every day more and more people are leaving for a new life in expanding Dublin suburbs. And where once the Square was alive with people, the death sentence has brought silence (*Evening Press*, 21 October, 1968).

With a few temporal changes to the script, such an epitaph could just as easily be written about the current situation in St.

Michael's Estate. Just as it does today, the proposal for a new estate in 1968 raised anxieties in the wider Inchicore area. There are remarkable parallels with the concerns of the adjacent estates then and now:

> Flats scheme angers residents. Residents at Connolly Avenue Inchicore, are angry over Dublin Corporation's proposals to build high rise, system built blocks of flats at the rear of their houses and also with the Corporation's silence in regard to the proposed development (*Evening Herald*, 15 January, 1969).

THE SOCIAL HISTORY OF THE ESTATE

The opening of the St. Michael's Estate in 1970 took place against the backdrop of a changing societal context. Ireland in the 1970s was slowly emerging from a lengthy period of economic and cultural isolation and was gradually embracing a new, expansionist ideology. The country was undergoing a late industrialisation and was experiencing the beginning of a period of economic growth and prosperity. It was within this changing historical milieu that St. Michael's Estate was opened. These broader social, economic and cultural factors would play a crucial role in the Estate's history over the coming years. When St. Michael's Estate opened in 1970s it housed a quintessential working class population. A sense of optimism and stability characterised the early years of the Estate. But a number of dynamics converged, some policy based, some larger macro-economic changes, which were to change the entire fabric of life on the Estate. In 1978, Dublin Corporation introduced a 'surrender grant' for residents in the city who wanted to buy their own homes and vacate their corporation flat. Tenants were offered a grant of five thousand pounds as a deposit toward the purchase of a first house. This was a positive incentive for those who had the means and motivation to take up the offer. But the grant scheme had a significant unintended consequence in that it profoundly weakened the social structure and networks of relationships on the Estate. This policy had the effect of destabilising the Estate and demoralising the remaining residents. Many of those with stable and secure incomes left the Estate for good. Allocations on the Estate into the future would increasingly be given to single parent families on low incomes. The grant scheme however, was only one dynamic among many. On a broader societal canvas, Ireland in the 1980s witnessed massive unemployment and emigration, and compounding this was the onset of a heroin epidemic amongst young people in working class communities in Dublin. Residents on the Estate found themselves caught up within a developing matrix of deprivation. The optimism of the early years was replaced by insecurity and fear, and gradually the Estate became a transient place with a high turnover of tenancies:

> The turnover of tenancies had detrimental effects for the Estate. It created an imbalance between young and old, single and married and employed and unemployed. The Estate became predominantly a place for single parents, many who suffered poverty and its effects. The 1980s saw the flats begin to deteriorate. Poor maintenance, broken lifts, vandalised flats, graffiti, crime, and drugs became the norm.[35]

Like many City Council estates, the complex turned in on itself as the Blocks themselves became miniature theatres of fear and intimidation over time. Given that the entrance to each Block was open plan there was complete and unfettered access from ground level to the internal stairwells, lifts and landings. Despite some attempts at securing the landings, the entrances and access points to landings remained virtually indefensible. Unwelcome visitors could be stopped from accessing landings from the stairs, but the lift system bypassed the landing doors and gave unrestricted access to each floor of the Block. The internal structure of the Blocks gives them a slightly claustrophobic feel. Beginning in the late 1980s and continuing into the 1990s, landings and internal spaces became commonly used as heroin shooting galleries. Maintaining the security of the Blocks and the safety of the residents became a difficult and dangerous task. Landings were plagued with unwanted strangers leaving trails of 'blood, vomit and excrement' at all hours of day and night. One clinical description of the Blocks portrayed them as 'human filing cabinets'.[36]

In May 1993, the Estate was designated for funding under the Remedial Works Scheme. A local working group was set up to ensure that the refurbishment of the Estate took place quickly. The working group was primarily driven by community organisations but there was also voluntary and statutory participation. A number of issues such as lighting, heating and the physical conditions of the Blocks themselves had been identified as priorities. However, despite urgent pleas by residents, community organisations and politicians, the work had still not begun by the middle of 1996. In the end the proposed work never took place. Frustrated with the chronic incapacity of the State to take action, the working group advocated urgently for the setting up of a new structure which would provide much needed energy and impetus:

> Despite the small scale improvements which were made in the last year the Estate is still in serious decline. This is now recognised by everyone. In recognising the level of deterioration and despair, it was decided that some positive action must be taken to exert some control over the destiny of the Estate and the people who live there....With this in mind, we applied to the Department of Environment and the Housing Management Initiative for funding to set up a special Task Force which would carry out research and compile a programme of action for the Estate which would give voice to the people of the Estate.[37]

The St. Michael's Estate Task Force was formally established in 1997 with an independent chairperson. The Task Force was composed of local tenants' representatives, community groups and organisations working on the Estate, Dublin City Council and other state agencies. The process of bringing together various 'sectors' and 'agencies' was a more formalised attempt at coming up with a strategy to deal with the neglect of the multi-layered issues on the Estate. Its key function was to look at strategies and possibilities for the future of the Estate. It would do this on the principle of integrating the combined resources and capacity of the community, voluntary and statutory sectors. From the Task Force came the idea that a consultation take place with residents as to their views on the possibilities for the future of the Estate. This took practical shape with the commissioning and publication of the *Consultation Document on the Future of St. Michael's Estate*. This document was an attempt at giving residents a democratic opportunity to decide on the future of the Estate.

This document was ostensibly written to seek residents' views about their preferred options for the future of the Estate. But it also contained a socio-economic profile of the Estate in 1998. The profile, while brief, revealed an Estate with an accumulation of deprivation including an endemic heroin problem, significant unemployment, an increasingly transient population and significant levels of educational disadvantage. The dominant image that emerged from the document was of an Estate cut off from mainstream Irish society. At this stage many of the newer tenants were coming to the Estate not with the intention of staying, but as part of a short term strategy of getting somewhere else. St. Michael's Estate wasn't a place to put down roots but instead became a stopover on the public housing caravan. Long term residents, who had been on the Estate since it was first constructed, found themselves gradually in a minority. Seventy per cent of those eligible for work were unemployed at this time. Of those that were working, all were "in the low paid areas of cleaning, catering, childcare, transport and clothing manufacture, which can all be stratified as unskilled manual".[38] The educational characteristics of the population reinforced, and to a great extent explained, the labour force positions; "overall the Estate exhibits a very low level of educational attainment amongst residents. This is clearly indicated by the fact that over 30 per cent describe themselves as early school leavers with no formal or educational qualifications".[39]

What the *Consultation Document* described most clearly was an estate in severe crisis. Residents saw no other alternative than to agree to have the Estate demolished. The most overt, primary reason given for this was the intensity of the heroin problem. Residents felt palpably intimidated and feared for the safety of their children and themselves:

> It was felt that the number of drug users resident on the Estate, combined with its reputation across the city as a point of sale for drugs led them very simply and straightforwardly to the conclusion that measures less radical than demolition would go nowhere towards ridding the Estate either of its reputation or the drugs problem itself. [40]

At the end of the consultation process, 64 per cent of residents stated, for all of the reasons outlined above, that their preference was for total demolition. For many of the tenants this was a very difficult decision to take. The flats on the Estate had been built to a high standard and were spacious in comparison to what was being built at the time in the city. Many had spectacular views from the upper floors. For those who would stay they would need all of the resilience and determination to see them through. One could become quietly melancholic when confronted with the harshness of St. Michael's Estate. But there has always been another side to the Estate which is one of spirit and a refusal to accept the social conditions as the way things had to be. The resilience of the people was not lost on the Chairperson of the St. Michael's Estate Task Force. In a foreword to the *Consultation Document*, he displayed a lucid understanding of the fact that, even in the grimmest of situations and the most marginalised of places, the possibilities for change exist:

> It is a commonplace assumption that among what we call 'opinion formers' there are no heroes in the world anymore. We are, we are told, limited and limiting. There is no one with a

vision, no one with courage, no one with commitment or a heart that never gives in. As far as the powerful, the significant and the influential go, all that is probably true.

Today's heroes live among the grassroots in the spaces ignored by the great and the vocal. They struggle with ignorance and with being ignored. They refuse to go into the boxes to which state and media consign them. And they never give in.

St. Michael's Estate is full of such heroes and heroines, people who are indestructible, and still full of hope, people who tolerated a lot, suffered too much but were never defeated by the State or by those whom the State allowed to come among them (*Brendan Ryan, Foreword to Consultation Document*, 1998).

After residents agreed to total demolition in 1998, the initial process began of working out how regeneration would happen and what it would look like. A project team was set up by Dublin City Council to oversee this first phase. The community sector lobbied to become part of this and was successful in gaining tenant participation on the team. However, it would prove a difficult and frustrating experience for residents. To participate effectively in its own regeneration, St. Michael's Estate would need to develop dynamic local structures and organisation. Regeneration would prove to be a complicated process which went far beyond the physical. However, St. Michael's Estate was perhaps unusual in one key respect in that it had built up a strong grassroots tradition of community work and development on the Estate over many years. Prior to getting into the heart of the regeneration process, we first need an understanding of these community development structures and organisations in St. Michael's Estate.

Chapter 4

A Brief history of Community Development in St. Michael's Estate

ST. MICHAEL'S ESTATE FAMILY RESOURCE CENTRE

It is the view of the Family Resource Centre that the growing inequality, poverty and exclusion, which characterise Irish society are linked closely to the structures by which our society is organised. To address these inequalities and divides we believe that action that involves those who experience exclusion, i.e. women, the unemployed, the working class, the gay community and Travellers are a priority in bringing about social change. [41]

In order to understand the community actors involved in the current regeneration process it is necessary to briefly sketch the history of community development work in St. Michael's Estate in recent years. There is perhaps no better place to start than with the local Community Development Project, the St. Michael's Estate Family Resource Centre (FRC). The FRC takes very seriously the view that inequalities in Irish society are a result of the way Irish society is structured. The FRC has committed itself, in its own small way, to changing this situation in which some groups have very little and others have almost limitless resources. This understanding informs and penetrates all aspects of the work in the project. The FRC was established in 1986 by local women and a Sister of Mercy living on the Estate as a response to issues of deprivation, poverty and marginalisation that were occurring on the Estate. The project 'opened a space for people to come together for laughter, for play, for struggle and to begin the process of community development' (Family Resource Centre, *Annual Report*, 1999: 9).

The FRC is primarily a women's community development project. The main office of the FRC is housed in a three bedroom City Council flat on St. Michael's Estate. Over the years, the project has expanded and now provides a range of community development, educational, artistic programmes and courses and more recently, outreach support services for women experiencing domestic violence. In 2004, the project moved from its original location in flat number 70, due to the first phase of demolition, to flat number 118 in Block Four of the complex. The project's flaming red hall door has developed something of a fame of its own and has become an enduring image and *leitmotif* of the project. The door acts as a practical aperture of welcome and hospitality in that it is an 'open door' to anyone wishing to enter. The red door also has a symbolic resonance as a metaphor for the defiance and refusal to accept glaring inequalities as being preordained, natural or acceptable. The door captures something of the resistance and spirit which animates the project and has done so since its inception. (The door was the signature image of the FRC in an international arts exhibition entitled 'Praxis' in Duluth, Minnesota in 2000.) The FRC has navigated a course through the haze of oppressions, that is part of daily life on the Estate and has done this from a position of solidarity with local people. The FRC has, from the outset, worked from a politicised community development model of practice:

> The role of the Family Resource Centre, through its commitment to community development, is to contribute to social change at local and national level. We see community devel-

opment as an alternative model of development, which enables and empowers local people to become active participants in the process to influence social, political, economic and cultural change. Our work is rooted in solidarity with those who experience social exclusion and is based on creating real partnerships that involve them.[42]

The FRC has done this using a variety of methods over the years. As well as the traditional methods of community development, the use of the arts as a medium for expressing the day to day lives of residents has become a unique characteristic of the project. The idea that the residents of St. Michael's Estate would engage in such a process, in itself challenged dominant conceptions as to who should do 'art' and how the subject matter of the arts should be determined. The themes of this work have been diverse and provocative. Domestic violence, the principals of community development and the subjective experience of daily life on the Estate have all been explored and exhibited using multi-layered artistic approaches. The use of the arts has undoubtedly been about exploring creative expression, but it has also made explicit political statements about the lives of those living on the Estate. Works made on the Estate have travelled extensively in Ireland and abroad and continue to provoke and to question. Asking questions and illuminating the nature of power and powerlessness is a recurrent and continuous theme of the project's work on the Estate:

> What is there, in the society and its structures that prevents the truth from coming to the fore? Why, when one would expect all communities experiencing inequalities to be stronger in their voice and also cause upheaval as a means to effect change – do they not do it? Is there something in how we, the community development movement have bought into the new structures of national partnership that prevents this question from being answered? ... What are the conditions we need to create when we are seeking to create a more equitable and just world and society?[43]

There are other community-based projects that have a significant relationship with the residents and the regeneration of St.
Michael's Estate. The St. Michael's Parish Youth Project was set
up in 1991 to work with young people living on the Estate and
in the surrounding parish. The youth project has been a core
organisation within the area since that time and continues to
work with young people at risk of serious drug use, educational
disadvantage and a host of other issues. The Inchicore Community Drug Team has a slightly more recent history and was set up
in 1998. The Drug Team is a central part of the Canal Communities Local Drugs Task Force Development strategy. The Drug
Team has responded primarily to the effects of opiate use in St.
Michael's Estate and the surrounding Inchicore community.
Both the Youth Project and the Drug Team are committed to
using community development as part of a more holistic
approach to tackling inequalities in the area.

THE ST. MICHAEL'S ESTATE BLOCKS' COMMITTEE

In parallel with the FRC, the actions of local residents have long
challenged the pessimistic view that the inequities facing them
are of a natural order of things. The order of things could be
changed. There has been a prolonged attempt by local people on
the Estate to shape their own lives and histories. The organisational initiative which most clearly epitomises this was the
establishment of the 'Blocks' Committee' on the Estate in early
1986. The establishment of this local organisation was an
attempt at mobilising local residents on the basis of issues facing
them within their individual blocks and also those facing the
complex as a whole. The origin of the group is described in the
Blocks' Committee's Annual Report from 1990-1991:

> In 1986 what was left of the old tenants association disbanded
> due to conflict amongst its members. This resulted in a new
> group being formed which named itself the Blocks' Commit-

tee. It is a voluntary group who meet on a weekly basis to discuss the problems of tenants on the Estate and to take action. Each individual tower or four storey block takes on responsibility for its own upkeep, block members deal with the authorities first. If support is needed they will call on the collective support of the Blocks' Committee. [44]

The Blocks' Committee has been centrally involved in the day to day work of community development now for over twenty years. The committee has had a symbiotic working relationship with the FRC and both organisations have mutually supported and consolidated each other. The FRC has nurtured the development of the Blocks' Committee from the employment of staff to work directly with tenants and residents, to providing spaces and hospitable conditions for meetings. The Blocks' Committee for its part has provided the conditions and space for the growth and development of a critical tenant consciousness. The Committee was the place where tenants brought forward the day to day issues that were absolutely critical to them. These were consistent material issues which have been at the heart of local struggles on the Estate including poor maintenance, safety and security, allocations policy, as well the overall physical conditions on the Estate. Given the rapid deterioration of the physical conditions, much of the work of the group throughout the 1990s was given over to an intense campaign for a thorough refurbishment programme for the Estate. There is something of *déjà vu* in the fact that a comprehensive physical plan was developed in the early 1990s to refurbish the existing Estate, but in the end only minor precinct improvements were made.

Sustaining community participation in the Blocks' Committee has proved difficult in recent years. The current process of regeneration, which effectively began in 1998, has proved to be hugely demanding on local people. This was especially the case in relation to the technical and architectural aspects of the process. Residents needed expert help and advice to interpret and to understand drawings and plans for the Estate. Given the proposed scale of regeneration, the Block's Committee sought support and solidarity in this process and early in 2001 invited a number of groups and individuals to become part of a Community Regeneration Team. This team would act as a support to the Blocks' Committee and residents throughout the regeneration process.

A COMMON APPROACH: A COMMUNITY REGENERATION TEAM

The formal establishment of the Community Regeneration Team occurred at a public meeting of residents in the local youth project in St Michael's Estate in May, 2001. The logic behind the Team was to gather together a pool of people and to use them as a resource to enable the residents on the Estate to contribute to, define and participate in the regeneration of the Estate. The Team would act as an advisory body to the Blocks' Committee and would not be a representative organisation on the Estate. The Community Regeneration Team was made up of local residents on the Estate, workers from community projects in and around the Estate, and workers/individuals from projects outside of the Estate. The Team has also been lucky enough to have been resourced by one of the most skilled architects working in the city of Dublin over the same period. Given the proposed scale of regeneration, some organisational form of response was going to be necessary if residents were not to be mere tokenistic bystanders in the process. Bringing such a group together, therefore, was designed to harness existing local capacity and other resources beyond the Estate. It was an attempt to support the residents of St. Michael's Estate to work their way through what would be an arduous and difficult process. Since February 2001, the Team has met on a weekly basis and has attempted to bring a rigour and a systematic approach to the process of regeneration.

Membership of the Team has changed over the years but a

core group has retained a sustained and intense involvement throughout the regeneration process. The emphasis focused on developing a dynamic collective approach where issues and ideas could be teased out and tested before being finalised and acted upon. The Team attempted to work out what a community-based vision of regeneration would look like. A good deal of energy also went into interpreting state proposals and devising appropriate responses. Over time, the Team has worked to reach common understandings on the possibilities for the Estate. It has worked on the basis that the sharing of ideas and energies is a far more useful way to approach the project than in an individualistic manner. The Team exploited individual resources in common and for a common end. A group may lack something of the creative genius of the individual but it more than makes up for this lack with increased energy and capacity. Groups also have the ability to refine things from multiple perspectives as opposed to only one. Often ignored or suppressed, groups have their own creativities.

One of the initial tasks of the Community Regeneration Team was the production of a position outlining what was important in regeneration from a community perspective. Subsequently, in 2002, *Past, Present and Future: A Community Vision for the Regeneration of St. Michael's Estate* was launched on the Estate. The document presented a realistic appraisal of the issues and argued that regeneration "treat St. Michael's Estate as a community and shall put forward a plan for the Estate which is holistic, integrated, comprehensive and which views the Estate in its entirety".[45] The document argued that for regeneration to work it needed to be multi-faceted and responsive to issues such as poverty, health, social housing and community participation. Lessons from other estates in Ireland and Britain had shown that physical transformation on its own was not enough. The underlying causes which brought the Estate to its current predicament needed to be addressed. *Past, Present and Future* was perhaps an inexperienced act of articulation but it was powerful nonetheless and provided a huge impetus to those living and working on St.

Michael's Estate. It became a general reference document to which the reality of regeneration was constantly contrasted. The document provided a blueprint of possibilities and was used as a community-based tool for navigating through the regeneration process. It was effectively a community work manifesto for regeneration.

This chapter has presented a short vignette of the history of community development on St. Michael's Estate in recent years. However, grassroots visions of regeneration developing in St. Michael's Estate would also have to contend with the perspective of the State. In the normal course of events managing such a process would be demanding in and of itself. But what happens when the State itself changes its entire regeneration paradigm in the middle of the process? It is to such a changed reality that we now turn.

Chapter 5

Changing Tracks:
The Authority of the State

I'll have my bond. I will not hear thee speak.
I'll have my bond, and therefore speak no more.[46]

O nce residents had expressed their preference for total
demolition in 1998, the first phase of regeneration effectively began to take place. This first phase encompassed
the building of two small schemes on sites adjacent to the Estate.
In the grounds of Goldenbridge Convent 51 housing units were
built, comprising a mixture of houses and apartments, while at
the Bulfin Road entrance, 50 housing units for older people were
also built. Both of these schemes were completed in 2001 and a
number of families and residents left St. Michael's Estate and
moved in. The blocks that were vacated as part of this first phase
were subsequently demolished in anticipation of the much larger
second phase of regeneration on the land of the Estate itself.

'MOVING AHEAD'

After this first phase was completed, Dublin City Council
launched a draft framework plan for the remainder of the Estate:

Dublin City Council yesterday unveiled a £60 million redevelopment

plan for St. Michael's Estate in Inchicore, Dublin, pledging it would transform the area into ' a very nice place to live'. Mr. John Fitzgerald, the city manager said local people had been 'very patient' while the plan was being prepared over the last twelve months. 'The last thing we want to do is to get it wrong and to have to do it all again in 10 years time' (*The Irish Times*, 13 June 2001).

The plan has been in development for three years and it is clear that Dublin City Council is hopeful it will proceed with tenant agreement. 'We cannot afford to run the risk of it going wrong,' said city manager John Fitzgerald. We have learned…the city owes the residents of St. Michael's a lot,' Fitzgerald said. 'We have accepted for a long time that the buildings were tainted' (*Sunday Business Post*, 17 June 2001).

The new framework plan for St. Michael's Estate was launched amid much fanfare in June 2001. The plan was progressively entitled 'Moving Ahead'. It was agreed by the St. Michael's Estate Task Force that a period of consultation be given over to hearing and recording residents' views on this new plan. Residents were subsequently given three months to debate the merits of the plan. The findings of the consultation process were written up in documentary form. A design sub-group of the Task Force was set up to oversee the development of the new plan. The sub-group was made up of representatives from the City Council, including the architectural team, residents, community organisations and local politicians. The 'Moving Ahead' plan evolved and became much more clearly defined as the issues that had been raised during the consultation were incorporated. Residents were kept informed as to the progress on the plan and were consulted regularly for their views and opinions. They began to take ownership of the plan and to shape it according to their needs. Final agreements on the plan were reached at a meeting on Good Friday afternoon in April 2003. All of those present were delighted with what had been achieved and congratulated each other. When finalised, the plan contained 320 housing units of which 150 were to be social, 80 housing units were to be affordable and 70 were to be private. The housing units were to be a mixture of traditional two and three storey housing, apartments, and duplex town houses. The plan also contained a range of community facilities and services for the Estate. The detail on the plan was at such an advanced stage that a group of landscape architects had been commissioned and had presented a fully detailed landscape design for the Estate by mid-2003. The public sections of the plan were to be funded through the State exchequer, while the affordable housing would be self financing. The private housing when sold would generate some revenue. Those residents who remained on the Estate at this stage expressed a high level of satisfaction with what had been achieved. They would get high standard accommodation, the new estate would be relatively low density, there would be play areas and facilities for their children, and the overall design of the site was done to a very high specification. An enormous amount of work had gone into achieving such outcomes. Residents felt strongly that they were indeed 'Moving Ahead'.

A SIGN OF THE TIMES: RENEGING ON THE PLAN

This plan was lodged for Planning Permission with An Bord Pleannala (The Planning Board) in the early Summer of 2003. There was a general air of excited anticipation at the prospect of new houses being built the following year and of the remaining residents being housed shortly thereafter. The St. Michael's Estate Task Force returned to session in September 2003 with the expectation that the plan had been passed and the process of implementation would now begin. However, at the first post-summer Task Force meeting a letter, that had been sent from the Department of the Environment to Dublin City Council in relation to the proposed plan, was presented to the St. Michael's Estate Task Force.

The following is an excerpt from the letter:

> The proposals for redevelopment were formulated a number of years ago and were the subject of a considerable level of public consultation. In the meantime the position on the ground has evolved considerably in that most of the tenants have been rehoused by the City Council. It is also the case that the financial climate in relation to public finances has changed considerably and we are facing more difficult times ahead. In this regard the Department is under a greater obligation to obtain optimum value for money. The Department has therefore reluctantly concluded that the proposed redevelopment in its current form cannot be supported.
>
> At this stage it is suggested that rather than the City Council revisiting the design, which will involve more time and resources being devoted to redesign with no certainty as to the outcome, that the possibility of a Public Private Partnership be explored for the redevelopment. This could produce a more satisfactory outcome in terms of the length of time for redevelopment and possibly at a lesser cost. This would also allow for a review of the breakdown of accommodation needs having regard to current circumstances. It would be appreciated, therefore, if this course of action were taken by the City Council.
>
> In conclusion the Department wishes to restate that it continues to be supportive of the City Council's decision to implement effective regeneration of the St. Michael's Estate area. (*Letter from the Department of the Environment to Dublin City Council read into the minutes at St. Michael's Estate Task Force*, 6 September, 2003).

This communication from the State had a variety of significances. It was a command from a distance, and the communication was anonymous, impersonal and bureaucratic. Whatever the process for reaching the conclusions above, there was no awareness or participation in it from the Estate itself. The idea that such a decision might somehow belong or be argued out amongst the relevant parties, including residents, was never countenanced. The content of the communiqué was broken locally at the beginning of September 2003. Ironically, the first time local people and members of community-based organisations heard about it, was at a meeting devoted to setting up new structures to oversee the implementation of the now rejected plan.

It was at this meeting that a city council official informed those present that the Department of the Environment had serious concerns about the economic viability of the 'Moving Ahead' plan given the current economic climate and the broader national context. The Department expressed the view that it was inappropriate to proceed with the planning option at this stage and stressed the need for all of the parties involved to explore the possibility of a Public Private Partnership (PPP) as an alternative to the 'Moving Ahead' plan. The proposal should therefore be re-examined using this new model.

In the Department's view, the principal issue was to derive the best value by using the skills of the private sector and thereby limiting the costs to the exchequer. The official stressed the point that the commitment to redevelopment maintained, only the means of achieving it has changed. The abrupt shift from one model to another made clear that local and central government, who had clearly been out of step with each other, were realigning their respective objectives into a much tighter, unilateral position.

A CHANGING FINANCIAL CLIMATE

A meeting was arranged between Dublin City Council, tenants and community organisations to resolve the impasse after the collapse of the plan. The meeting took place in a converted flat on the Estate which houses the Family Resource Centre. The chairs were locked together in a tight circle given the combination of a small room and a large group. There was expectation on the community side that the issue could be resolved and that there had to be some way of reinstating the 'Moving Ahead' plan. However, it became clear that the City Council, on instruction from the Department had moved into a completely new mode of regeneration. At the outset of the meeting officials made a strong case that housing the 'remaining tenants' was a priority for the City Council. There were sixty five tenants still left on the estate at this stage. The Council would also attempt to provide some community facilities. But, the 'Moving Ahead' plan was effectively a thing of the past and the money just wasn't there any more to do such a plan. Officials argued that within a changed financial climate money was tighter and tighter, and PPP offered opportunities that hadn't previously existed. By using the model of PPP there would be more than just money for housing, but also for childcare and other community facilities. The workings of PPP were explained, suggesting that the City Council would give the site for nothing and in turn the social housing and community facilities would be built for nothing. At this stage most of those present had little or no idea how PPP would actually work in practice.

Upon direction from the Department of the Environment, the City Council had quickly adopted the framework of PPP for the regeneration of St. Michael's Estate. What surprised most people was the abruptness with which the State changed tracks. Perhaps even more important was the sense that the change was non-negotiable. The entire regeneration process had been rerouted on to a new line. The way that regeneration would happen and how it would be done had been altered fundamentally by a change of economic model. The plan that had been developed over the previous two years was to have been financed primarily through public funding. The financial structuring of regeneration under PPP would be radically different to that of a State-funded project. There had been very few public housing projects on City Council land that had used this model, but the position was obviously changing.

In this instance, the City Council was the bearer and articulator of this sea change. This rationale contained a justification for changing track and yet, even at this early stage, the import and consequences of such a change was becoming clear. The 'commitment to house the remaining tenants', was a departure from existing understandings between the community and the City Council. Residents had explicitly declared their preference that the Estate be used primarily for a City Council housing scheme when they had agreed to demolition in 1998. But from the time agreement on demolition had been reached, the City Council had pursued a policy of not retenanting flats as tenants moved off the Estate. The absolute numbers of tenants living in occupied flats was, therefore, always in continuous decline. At the time when the Department of the Environment recommended PPP, there were sixty-five tenants remaining on the Estate. However, in the plan the Department of the Environment had rejected, there had been a commitment to provide one hundred and seventy social housing units. The sentiment of the City Council and the Department to rehouse remaining tenants, while appearing eminently altruistic was a first strike at ensuring the numbers of social housing be minimised.

The changing financial climate was used as justification for rejecting the plan that had been almost two years in the making and the result of intense collaboration between the community and State. The complex economic logic of PPP was also presented in simplified format, giving the impression that "we give the site for nothing and the social housing and community facilities will be built for nothing". This changeover to PPP shows the Irish State in something of a different light. This is the State as trader, entrepreneur and capitaliser of assets. For PPP to take place, the City Council needed to undertake a feasibility study in order to ascertain the value of the land. The value of the land was perhaps the critical factor in the structuring of any potential PPP project. On more than one occasion the metaphor of 'tapping the value' of the land was used to describe how such an extraction would take place.

To the Department and officials, PPP provided the perfect release mechanism for such value. Time and again during this period the mechanism of PPP was hailed as the most expeditious way of doing a project like this. PPP would be faster and much more cost efficient than any other model of regeneration. PPP could also help stimulate the commercial heart of the area of Inchicore in that it could potentially provide a hotel or a supermarket on the front of the site.

However, even at this early stage it was clear that PPP would impose certain conditions. The limiting of social housing was perhaps the most important of these. What emerges here is the changing role of the City Council and a new approach to its tenants and land banks. The framework of PPP would be the State's solution to poverty and deprivation, its formal retort to the tortured question as to what process and mechanism could transform and change an estate like St. Michael's. In practical terms this would come through the social restructuring of the Estate and also through the extraction of value from the land. This needed to happen because, according to the City Council, St. Michael's had found itself caught up in a confluence of factors, principal of which was the vicarious nature and unpredictability of the Irish economy. In the boom years of the Celtic Tiger lots of projects had been approved such as Ballymun and Killarney Court. But the bubble had now burst according to officials and St. Michael's Estate was going forward for planning at the worst time in the past ten years. PPP offered a better, quicker and cheaper way of doing regeneration and from the council's perspective, 'there is no other option but PPP'.

In early November 2003 the *Irish Times* ran a story with the headline '€63 million plan for estate dropped as council sells site.' Somewhat prematurely, the reporter concluded "Dublin City Council has abandoned plans to redevelop one of the city's most deprived areas, St. Michael's Estate in Inchicore, because of a lack of money. Instead the council intends to sell the lucrative 11-acre site to private developers, who will be required to provide some social housing in a public-private partnership." The article stoked the fears and insecurities of residents and organisations on the Estate who sought clarification from the City Council as to what would happen next. The reporter did pick up on one important facet of the PPP process and one which would recur again and again when he concluded "the less social housing the site contains, the more valuable it is to a developer and the less the ultimate cost to the council" (*Irish Times*, 3 November 2003). In a somewhat surreal coincidence, the *Irish Times* ran another article on the same page heralding the arrival of the new Dublin City logo. The new logo, set against a sky blue background, with the city's new landmark spire soaring through its centre read 'Dublin: make the city yours' (*Irish Times*, 3 November 2003).

SUMMARY: PREPARING THE GROUND FOR PPP

Almost overnight, Dublin City Council had changed its entire method of approach to the regeneration of St. Michael's Estate. On the back of the recommendation for PPP they began to liaise directly with a new set of architects in the development of a new masterplan. There would be no co-operative design structures where local residents or community organisations would participate in the plan's definition. The plan would be produced in isolation from the St. Michael's Estate Task Force and would be presented for 'consultation' very much as a *fait accompli*. During the development of this new plan there was only a token acknowledgement of the Task Force. The City Council informed the Task Force that the practicalities of PPP now needed to begin. The City Council was beginning its feasibility study in relation to costing the value of the land in order to bring a proposal to the Public Private Benchmarking body. This was being done to discover the value and cost which would be derived from a PPP.

The changeover to PPP had been delivered by decree. It had the feeling of an electric shock, especially to the residents of St. Michael's Estate. This decree would have a huge effect on them and their families for it effectively meant starting all over again from scratch. From the State's perspective the change was entirely justifiable. It had given its own rationale and justification and stated that there was no other option. Like it or not, it had to be PPP.

Chapter 6

The Development of a Community Resistance

> …the poor embody the ontological condition not only of resistance but also of productive life itself…despite their poverty and their lack of material resources, food, housing, and so forth, the poor do have an enormous wealth in their knowledges and powers of creation.[47]

> For always, no matter how powerful one's armies, in order to enter a country one needs the goodwill of the inhabitants.[48]

THE PAINFUL EFFECTS OF POWER

The rejection of the plan had a profound emotional effect on local people on the Estate. Residents who had watched the 'Moving Ahead' plan grow and take shape were stunned. As a result, many of those who still lived on the Estate left over a period of time. They had spent a lot of energy and time commenting on successive drafts of the plan and had a general idea as to where they would be housed on the site. The locations of social, affordable and private housing on the site had been established as had the type and size of housing residents would get. The design was at such an advanced stage that the landscaping plan was almost complete down to public benches and installations. Residents had psychologically internalised the plan and had been preparing themselves for the beginning of construction. The breach of trust and faith induced a palpable anxiety. It also left residents in an extremely vulnerable position with no real certainty as to their futures. There was confusion and desperation at what had occurred and bewilderment that it could happen at all. Residents who had become hopeful for their futures were quietly devastated.

Shortly after the rejection of the plan a public meeting was held for residents of the Estate. The meeting had been called and organised by the Community Regeneration Team. Almost fifty residents, mainly women, many with children, showed up to be updated on the information which had been given to the Task Force meeting. The word was out on the street and while residents knew roughly what had happened they weren't sure why the plan was rejected or what could be done about it. A number of those who had moved off the Estate in the first phase of regeneration into the newly-built adjacent estates of Emmet Crescent and Bulfin Court also came to the meeting. There was a strong sense of solidarity between those left on the Estate and those who had already got their new housing. This meeting was planned around the ideas of informing people, of reassuring and minding them and of looking for a way forward.

Rita Fagan, a member of the Community Regeneration Team, chaired the meeting and opened by saying "If we stick together as a community we have a much better chance of succeeding". Martin Carroll, a local resident and also a member of the Regeneration Team read out a copy of the by now infamous letter. He used the phrase 'not economically viable' (echoing the local official from the City Council) to describe the State's position on the 'Moving Ahead' plan for the Estate. This phrase became the shorthand for describing the State's rejection and refusal to fund the plan. Eilish Comerford, a local community worker, took people through the component parts of the plan that had been rejected. Many of the residents and local Blocks' Committee members had brought with them their own coloured copies of this plan that they had been given at previous regeneration meetings. They appeared like totems, spread around the room. Residents shared a small number of plans out amongst themselves as Eilish explained the location and content of the various schemes within the plan. In small groups the anxieties of residents were clear. One local woman confided "I want out of the flats but I don't have enough points for a transfer", while another was adamant that she "couldn't wait any longer with nowhere for the kids to play or anythin". Another woman said she would "wait for two years if she knew that her house would be built". She showed little outward confidence that this would happen. The idea of looking for solutions from local people was somewhat overshadowed by their immediate concerns and fears. The rejection of the plan had brought to light how little control residents had over their own destiny. Time was everything to people as they weighed up their options as to whether they could hold on or seek a move off the Estate. The rejection of the plan and its consequences raised deep existential anxieties for them and their families. A strong sense of incapacity hung over the room.

Gradually, however, over the course of the meeting, a shift occurred, imperceptible at first, but it began to take shape around a more positively-oriented view. A way forward began to emerge around the idea that the rejected plan could and would be reinstated. The residents were supportive of the idea of campaigning to get the plan back on the table. At the end of the meeting Rita Fagan, a community worker who has worked on the Estate since the mid-1980s, unexpectedly, began to speak the phrase 'the plan agreed is the plan delivered' in a soft, mantra-like fashion. Residents in the room picked this up, slowly at first, as if they were joining up the links in the chain. The phrase began to ripple out around the room. Like a chorus of sorts, it spread around until almost all of those present were softly chanting the phrase, 'the plan agreed is the plan delivered'. Behind the shock and hurt, there was a quiet determination in the voices. Residents in the room retained a glimmer of belief in the plan and their housing.

A COMMUNICATIONS STRATEGY

Soon afterwards, the Community Regeneration Team established a local Campaign Group to work specifically on reinstating the rejected plan. The Campaign Group was a mixture of existing Regeneration Team members and new people who had come on board. One of the initial actions of the Campaign Group was the drawing up of a letter that would go out to all of the relevant local and national newspapers. The letter contained an overview of the situation and was a first attempt to draw wider attention to what had happened:

> A plan was drawn up which was agreed upon by all of the relevant sectors as imaginative, forward thinking, perhaps even visionary. The plan was developed on a holistic basis and not just around housing but also from a social, cultural, economic and environmental perspective…we are being told by the State that the plan is not economically viable. What we would like to know is where did the money go? Many questions are already appearing on the horizon and perhaps most prominent among them is the provision of housing by the State for families who have no access to the private housing market (Letter drafted by St. Michael's Estate Campaign Group for the media, 19 September 2003).

As part of an attempt to bring attention to what was happening the letter was wholly ineffective. It was never published by any of the mainstream or local newspapers. The letter's failure to penetrate the public sphere forced a rethink. If a message could not be disseminated to the wider public through orthodox media outlets, how would the community of St. Michael's Estate communicate what had happened? How could the public in general be informed about recent events? The rejection of the plan had forced the Regeneration Team to ask; what is it that we want to say; what is the message? After some arduous and difficult sessions some core ideas emerged. They were rough and unpolished and formed around the themes promoting the retention of social housing, low-rise housing, a low density development and a strong community. The 'Moving Ahead' plan that had been rejected by the State, contained almost all of these elements. The converse of this was the opposition to a high-rise, high-density development from a community perspective, for example, planning proposals for some sites in the city had a ratio of 120 housing units to one acre of land. The defining and publicising of a community position was at the core of this. There was an idea that messages would be located on billboards in the area. However, the capacity to do this work and to do it effectively was weak in St. Michael's Estate. The community had very little financial or other resources to build and sustain a wider media campaign which would have clear and powerful effects.

And yet, through word of mouth, what had happened was slowly filtering out into other communities and local development circles. Discussions of the issue took place in many forums and networks. At one of these, the suggestion was put forward that St. Michael's Estate needed to 'reflect, analyse, discuss and act' on what had happened. This phrase contains within itself the core aspects of community work practice. It could be described as the community work 'wheel' or 'cycle'. The idea posed many questions and challenges, not least of which was plotting the journey across this new terrain. While residents and local organisations were determined to respond, how to do it was still to be worked out. The community was still very much in the early stages of reflection and discussion. This changed with the contact and subsequent engagement with a communications company in the heart of the city.

IDENTITY, MESSAGE, METHOD

> Messages have to be compelling and they have to tell a story (John Sutton, Public Communications Centre, 12 December, 2003).

Behind an anonymous black hall door on one of Dublin's busiest inner city streets lies the Public Communications Centre ('a creative communications resource for progressive non-profits' is its concise mission statement). Once inside there is a staircase ahead at the end of a long hall and as one ascends there are a number of framed posters that are the stock in trade of the company. In fact, the entire structure of the building is an Aladdin's cave of image and visual provocation. The walls of the building change, chameleon like, over time as new images are added. Such images reveal something of the identity of the company and perhaps of its politics and value system. They act as a visual, public curriculum vitae. Many of the images have been used as part of public campaigns and refer to groups and issues that are generally outside of the mainstream of Irish and international societies. Coming here was an entry into the unusual world of public communications. Understanding and working in this milieu took some time to adjust to, for it was unfamiliar and had its own set of rules, language and internal logic. The relationship which was to develop here was to be critical to the community-based regeneration of St. Michael's Estate and marked something of a departure from the traditional political responses to issues of power and powerlessness. At our first meeting, almost before we were seated, we were asked, 'Who are you? Who is doing the talking here? What is it that you want to say? Who do you want to say it to? What do you want to achieve?'

The questions were asked by the managing director of the company John Sutton, who, along with a team of staff, would work collaboratively with St. Michael's Estate over the coming months. The questions encapsulate all aspects of communication from the identity of the messenger to the functions of the message; Who was speaking here? What was our identity? Was it residents or community organisations or a mixture of both? Who would own and author whatever was produced as part of this process? Beyond questions of identity, were questions of substance and content. Given that Dublin City Council was in the process of developing a brand new plan how would the community respond? It was clear from the public meeting on the Estate that the reinstatement of the original 'Moving Ahead' plan was the simplest objective. We were shown an 'information pack' off the shelf at this first meeting as an example of what a tangible communications product looked like and while showing it John Sutton stated the need for clarity and impact:

> We need to think of the audiences and prioritise. What are we saying to planners, Inchicore residents, City Councillors? What do we want them to do? We need to identify the key audiences and messages. We need to give a lot of thought to our objective. We need to find ways of talking that will grab people's attention (Communications meeting, PCC, 10 November 2003).

Over a period of time a set of objectives gradually crystallised and firmed up. One of the core objectives was to redress clear inequalities of respect in the relationship between the community and the State. The communications strategy would attempt to create the conditions for real and meaningful negotiations between the community of St. Michael's Estate, Dublin City Council and the Department of the Environment. This highlighted implicit inequalities in the structuring of relationships as they currently stood. A broad set of audiences would be targeted ranging from those in positions of political power to residents of the wider Inchicore area. A message gradually took shape around reinstating the Moving Ahead plan that had been rejected. It was within this context that the importance of social housing to the entire regeneration project was being consolidated and reinforced.

The process of clarifying objectives, audiences and message formed the beginnings of an outline for a 'communications plan'. The plan evolved to contain a small number of critical elements. The first of these had to do with developing materials and images that would be used locally to inform and to educate people as to what had happened and to seek their support. Allied with this was the idea of formally analysing the economics of the regeneration of St. Michael's Estate. In many ways this was an attempt to counter the dominant state-driven economic perspective. Within the third element was an effort to use the knowledge of regeneration both in Ireland and internationally in a practical fashion. The final part of the communications plan had to do with getting support and endorsement for the community position from 'influentials'. The development of a communications plan was an attempt to build a multi-layered body of information, materials and knowledge that would provide the foundations for a community-based campaign. Behind the strategy was an attempt to increase community influence and power:

> To be as strong as possible in the room you need to light fires outside the room. You are never quite sure which action is going to achieve which outcome so you've gotta do them all. Light as many fires as you can and don't take just one message. Diversify. Its all about perceptions. If they perceive you to be strong and bullish it changes things. Its about influencing the influencers. Who influences the decisions makers? No one is an island. The City Manager or anyone. If you can find a route in that's the way to go (John Sutton, Communications Meeting, PCC, 2 November, 2003).

Over the course of the work with PCC, a number of what could best be described as 'Campaign Stories' were told at different times. They were part of the histories of other disputes and campaigns both at home and abroad. They were listed as successful examples of where communications made a difference. It was within this context that it was said that 'community activists know how to oppose, but they don't know how to win'. The campaign stories were about many things, not least of which was winning, and they had clear resonances with the experience of St. Michael's Estate. The following are three summaries of such campaign stories:

> The workers in Team Aer Lingus were getting a hard time in the dispute. They were losing. It was discovered that European

airlines and African airlines owed 17.5 million pounds in unpaid fees for work that had been done on their aircraft. When the chief executive of Team Aer Lingus was confronted with this information by Charlie Bird of RTE the message changed from inefficient workforce to inefficient management.

The Ebro river in Barcelona was being dammed upstream and it was going to cause considerable problems and distress for communities living in Barcelona. So the local people decided that they would make a stand against this. They started the Blue Bus campaign where over 6,000 people travelled on these blue buses to the European Union to protest at what was happening. The reason they took the fight to Brussels was that the EU was funding 40 per cent of the project so they would have a key influence on policy in Spain.

Chinese women in San Francisco were not accessing breast cancer screening programmes. Someone noticed that they shopped for fresh food every day. They then put the information on screening programmes in rice bags and within a short time large numbers of Chinese women were accessing breast cancer screening programmes. Having the right message is important but just as important is how you deliver it.

At critical junctures in each of these cases something happened to change a course of events that otherwise seemed fixed. In each case, the use and content of communications was critical to the change occurring. Perhaps the critical point was that communications can and should take multiple forms. Throughout the work with PCC there was an attempt to devise an image that would convey the essence of what had happened in St. Michael's Estate. Over time, many images and ideas were explored. But a defining image gradually took shape of the sole of a large boot stamping down over an underlaid photograph of residents of the Estate. The text on the poster read 'Don't let the City Council Stamp on our Plan'. The footprint carried within it other, more subliminal messages of authority and power. The image, a form of which can be seen on the cover of this book, came to be the centerpiece of the communications strategy and was the principal image of community resistance. It was given the nickname 'Bigfoot'. The image appeared on every piece of campaign material from posters, to t-shirts, to campaign packs to banners. It was the central symbol on the petition document that went into every household in Inchicore seeking the reinstatement of the plan.

LAUNCHING A CAMPAIGN

It had taken almost six months to do it, but on the 26 April 2004 a formal, public campaign was launched in St. Michael's Estate to have the 'Moving Ahead' plan reinstated. The plan was rechristened 'The Community Plan' as part of the communications strategy. A huge public banner had been made with the Statement 'Save the Community Plan' stamped in red capital letters against a yellow background. It was close to twenty feet across and three feet tall and was book ended on each side with the Bigfoot image and text. The banner was strung out across the exterior wall of block three. The launch took place in beautiful Spring sunshine. A cable was fed through the window of the Family Resource Centre and a microphone stand with podium was set up. Chairs were set out in front of the podium for people. As the morning went on a large number of people began to gather for the event. Almost everyone present was given a T-shirt which had the 'Save the Community Plan' statement on the front and the Bigfoot image on the back. Nearly all of the residents present were wearing these. A number of radio stations were present as were RTE who carried a section about the launch on the main evening news later in the day.

Eilish Comerford, a community worker on the Estate, opened the proceedings by saying "We had a really good plan for this Estate which was rejected last September and this is what has brought us here today. We aren't going to take it lying down, we're fighting back now". Many of the women who were left on the Estate were sitting in the front row as she introduced P.J. Drudy, a well known Irish economist, to the large crowd. He spoke of the numbers on housing waiting lists nationally and in Dublin and of the City Council selling off its 'crown jewels' – the land. He described the St. Michael's Estate as "a place of vast possibilities, educational, housing, sporting perhaps even a new swimming pool. A new town could be built here. But it is not just about the physical. It is really about the other side to regeneration." Martin Carroll, a local resident who had grown up on the Estate came next to the podium and said "We have a good plan. The Department of the Environment abandoned it and marginalised us. We are coming back with this campaign to inform, to educate and to raise awareness". He thanked people for attending.

A bus had been organised to take anyone who wanted to go to the City Council Civic Offices to make a public statement of the campaign launch on the steps of the Wood Quay building. The purpose was to lodge a copy of the campaign pack with the City Manager and the Assistant City Manager for Housing. There was a vibrant energy on board as the bus traveled toward the civic offices. All on board were wearing the Bigfoot T-shirt, everyone seemed to be blowing whistles and everyone had a copy of the poster in their hands as they disembarked from the bus. A large group assembled on the steps of the City Council looking out over the river Liffey. Chants that had begun on the bus continued for a time on the steps of the City Council Civic Offices on Wood Quay. A number of the national newspapers were there to take photographs.

Campaign posters went up in the windows of flats on the Estate and houses all over Inchicore and beyond. The idea of the poster as a public statement of defiance was bolstered by the more substantial aspect of a petition which went into every household in Inchicore requesting that residents endorse the position for the reinstatement of the rejected plan. Going from door to door, the general feeling one got was that the people of Inchicore were anxious about the newly proposed plan that Dublin City Council was in the process of developing and were deeply unhappy with the shape and scope of it. In the end some 3,500 signatures were recorded through the petition and were duly lodged, bow and ribbons attached, to the office of the Dublin City Manager, 30 June, 2004.

Another element of the communications strategy was the production and distribution of a document which began to explore the new relations being engendered by PPP. The piece, aptly entitled *Changing Partners*, asked 'whether the Public Private Partnership model has now replaced the State-Community Partnership model as the accepted framework for the regeneration of residential urban areas'.[49] This work added to the momentum being developed in St. Michael's Estate and explored the implications of PPP from a social policy perspective. In particular, it posed questions around the use, control and sale of state assets, the further alienation of local communities, and the State's commitment to the participation of local communities in their own regeneration.[50]

PLAN B: THE CITY COUNCIL DEVELOPS A NEW FRAMEWORK PLAN

Almost as soon as the 'Moving Ahead' plan had been rejected, Dublin City Council had begun to develop a brand new, framework masterplan for the Estate in collaboration with a team of architects. There had been no participation or input from residents or community organisations into this new plan. This framework plan was officially unveiled during the early summer of 2004 for a period of 'consultation' with residents and local groups. The scale of the new plan shocked people. There were now 850 housing units and the size of the site had increased to 14 acres. A three acre site adjacent to the Estate and fronting on to Emmet Road had been included in this new plan. This three acre site housed a number of buildings including a small health centre, the local parish community centre (6,000 square feet), the local pigeon club building and a Travellers' halting site. A number of the blocks of apartments on the plan were seven/eight stories in height. No conventional two or three storey housing appeared on the plan. All of the housing units were to be apartments with a small number of duplexes. There were a small number of community facilities. The plan went on public display for a very brief number of sessions in Bulfin Court Community Centre and then in the Oblates Centre in Inchicore. At a public meeting the St. Michael's Estate residents were startled by the scale of the proposed plan. Referring to the lack of housing, one resident said "what's gonna happen to me? I was offered a two bedroom house". Another resident, who was a mother with four children responded to the plan by saying "It's highrise again, and there's too many apartments." Another of the women said "they're disgraceful, absolutely disgraceful. We're movin' out of highrise and here you have people livin' over you again."

There was a sense of disbelief at how completely out of touch this new framework plan was with their wishes. When asked what it was that they wanted residents responded forcefully by saying 'houses with front and back gardens, a choice of housing and not to be stuck in one little corner of the Estate'. At wider consultation sessions the reception was almost as hostile. One of the most serious critiques was around the consultation process itself. If a resident or interested individual wanted to make a comment on the plan it had to be written or typed and lodged on the night or by post. This method of consultation was submission-based and neglected (deliberately or not) the way that the residents of the Estate would naturally communicate their thoughts and feelings on what they were seeing. Culturally it was a method that did not fit the place. Most people responded orally to what they were seeing and made comments ranging from deep and prolonged to short summations of what they saw. The problem was that none of this would be recorded and therefore would not be responded to. The only formal record of consultation would be what was written down, and lodged as a formal comment. Very few people made written consultation contributions.

The unveiling of this newly developed framework plan coincided with the demolition of Blocks One, Two and Three on the front of the site. As the City Council's new plan was in circulation the demolition company had moved on to the site. A machine with a telescopic arm slowly stripped each of the blocks piece by piece, working from the summit to the base. The eight storey building that was Block Three was stripped bare over a few days revealing the innards of the structure and with it the decorative taste of those families who had lived there for many years. The interiors were revealed, opening a momentary vista to the lives of a generation.

LOCAL POLITICS: A PUBLIC MEETING IN INCHICORE

Watching people make their way to the hall that summer's evening gave Inchicore the aura of a country village where something vital was about to happen. People were converging from all directions toward the Parish Centre, which, on this night, possessed a curious, hallucinatory magnetism drawing in all and sundry from all corners of the area. The layered histories of families and friends revealed themselves with acknowledgements and intimate greetings. Over the course of the evening a sense emerged of families that had lived here for generations and were struggling to come to terms with a massive physical and social change to their landscape. On the night, Inchicore presented itself publicly as a concerned community, energised and vociferous, engaging frantically with this current phase of its history and attempting to shape and influence the development on St. Michael's Estate. All of the things that characterise a community were present; roots, relationships, intimacy, and care. Perhaps it was the history and the lineage of the people, their rootedness and sense of place, that was most striking on this night. The meeting was the culmination of months of door stepping work that had been carried out by members of the Community Regeneration Team Campaign Group and the

Blocks' Committee from the Estate. They had doggedly canvassed the streets of Inchicore over a sustained period of time. All of this work had prepared the ground for the night's meeting. Most of those who attended the meeting had received a copy of the campaign pack informing them of the nature of the debate taking place on the Estate. They had also had the opportunity to see what the City Council was proposing for the Estate in the form of its new framework plan. This meeting had been called by the St. Michael's Estate Campaign Group to support the residents still living on the Estate.

This was a night when the informal politics of community development flared up and fused with wider city politics. All of the local political representatives and some from the national arena were present. It was a moment when Inchicore appeared to wake from a soporific slumber. This meeting was one of the largest gatherings in the area for some years and had been planned to give public expression to the frustration around the new Dublin City Council framework plan and to highlight what had happened in recent times. There was a restless tension in the hall prior to the start of the meeting. Two members of the campaign group, Michael O' Flanagan and Rita Fagan co-chaired the meeting. The meeting was highly energised but well disciplined. The room crackled with this energy throughout with people striving to have their say. After a brief explanation of recent history and the City Council's new framework plan, individuals in the audience spoke in brief interval pieces of their anxieties about what was coming on stream. Some urged those present to participate in the modification and reform of the new framework plan:

> … fill in the comment sheets for Dublin City Council. You go into the office and you fill out the comment sheet and add in what you think. This is the last time to get it right. They are taking away the library and the hall and they are giving nothing it their place for what they're taking away. We'll be back in fifteen years with the same problems (Frank Hayes, Local Inchicore Resident).

A woman who had spent all of her life living on St. Michael's Estate maintained that the really important issue here was the remaining residents and their future prospects, for in all of this, it was they who were really being neglected:

> .... it's a shame that people are left in the conditions that they are.... people here know that we had a campaign against St. Pats (local League of Ireland football club) when they wanted the land to build a football stadium and looking back it might have been better if we had agreed because the residents might have got their houses that way. The residents are not getting what they were promised, the lifts are not being maintained and people have no pipe television cos the pipe company won't go up the blocks....the plan is a sham, residents are entitled to their houses, no questions asked, with front and back gardens (Ann Marie Brennan, St. Michael's Estate Resident).

What was clear to all of those who were present in the hall on this night was that there was little or no support for the City Council's new framework plan. The political representatives present were given their moment in the limelight at the end of the meeting to have their say. As happens at such events there is always a degree of populist playing to the gallery by politicians. Councillors urged people to use the formal political system in order to resolve this issue. According to politicians, the energy and opposition generated tonight would only be useful if it passed through the formal political channels of the City Council:

> I want to say a little bit about the residents of St. Michael's Estate who have been left on their own. It is time that we demand, not ask, that they be given their houses....I'm here as a resident and a public representative. This plan can't go ahead. We need to lobby the 52 City Councillors. They will make the final decision (City Councillor, Catherine Byrne).

> I support the original plan of the Task Force. The government has a policy of divide and conquer. There has to be a lobby of the fifty-two City Councillors. You need to ask councillors to

openly pledge their support for your position. The best of luck
with the campaign (City Councillor Joan Collins).

At the end of the meeting in the local parish hall a motion
was put to the floor asking those present were they against or in
favour of Dublin City Council's new framework plan. A sea of
hands were raised against. There was not one hand in support.

CITY POLITICS

As the ermine-clad Lord Mayors from previous eras looked
down upon the new, state of the art City Council chamber, a
motion was put to the floor of Dublin City Council on the new
framework plan. The energy and momentum that had been
created by the public campaign had created the conditions for
such a motion to occur. It was clear from the public meeting in
Inchicore that there was a critical mass of public resistance to the
City Council's new plan. The motion was a direct challenge to
the institutional objectives of the officials of Dublin City Council
in St. Michael's Estate:

> I call on the members of the (City) Council to unanimously
> reject the (new City Council framework) plan on the grounds
> of no proper consultation… I am urging the council to reject
> this plan and give people a real future. I am calling on all parties
> to support this. We have seen the demolition of Ballymun
> where people have got their houses and while the gardens may
> not be big they have their privacy. People in St. Michael's Estate
> want the same. We need to say we have made the right decision.
> The groups behind me (the St. Michael's Estate Blocks'
> Committee and Community Regeneration Team) have worked
> tirelessly (City Councillor Catherine Byrne, City Hall Council
> Chamber 6 September 2004).

In the Council Chamber all 52 City Councillors were present as
were the Dublin City Manager and the Assistant City Manager

for Housing. The incumbent Lord Mayor, Michael Connaughton, also from Inchicore, and Chair of the City Council had opened the meeting. Residents and members of the St. Michael's Estate Blocks' Committee and Community Regeneration Team sat in the public gallery and watched the proceedings unfold with intense interest. Earlier in the evening there had been sharp exchanges between City Councillors and the City Manager over the proposed sale of thousands of City Council flats in Dublin to tenants. One councillor had put forward a motion that this sale would not go ahead unless a process of consultation took place between all of the respective stakeholders. The motion on St. Michael's Estate took place within this increasingly politicised context of housing and social change in the city. With the motion being put, representatives from political parties and independent councillors were given time to air their views on the motion and the current context on the Estate:

> The original plan was bottom up. The community put a lot of social capital into it. They were devastated. This is a slow process of depopulation. We should support the local community who put social regeneration at the top of the agenda (City Councillor Mick Rafferty).

> The balance has not been struck here. I live in a complex where there is a good balance between housing and facilities. It's a good place to live. In this plan the balance has not been struck (City Councillor Charlie Ardagh).

> I want to note the positive campaign that has been run by residents over the past number of months. We fully support the motion. There was not enough consultation on the draft plan. Where public houses are demolished they should be replaced (City Councillor Andrew O Connell).

> The essence of a city is the interrelationship between the people, officials and bureaucracy. We need to rethink this strategy. I want to support the motion (City Councillor Bill Tormley).

The City Manager, not a little indignant at what was happening, suggested that many in the Chamber hadn't even seen the plan and went on to say that there had been a huge amount of consultation. He proposed that the Lord Mayor convene the relevant groups and parties with the assistance of an independent facilitator. Councillor Catherine Byrne responded by saying, "I want to put it to a vote to reject the plan." Almost a year to the day after the 'Moving Ahead' plan had been rejected by the Department of the Environment, all fifty two Dublin City Councillors voted unanimously to reject the City Council's new framework plans for St. Michael's Estate. The City Manager and the Assistant City Manager for Housing were clearly angry with the outcome and left the building hurriedly. Through the development of a sustained campaign, residents and community organisations in St. Michael's Estate had successfully challenged the City Council, and momentarily at least, had won. The impossible had become the improbable until it eventually became the possible. John Sutton's thesis that community activists know how to oppose but not how to win had also taken a battering. St. Michael's Estate had won. For now.

Chapter 7

The Realpolitik of PPP

In an unusual reversal of roles, Dublin City Council was now in the position of spurned suitor with its plans in tatters. Its initial response was to retreat into a defensive and hostile position as it found itself on uncertain, shaky ground. Given that all of the political representatives at the City Council had voted to reject the framework plan it was not only publicly embarrassing, it also raised serious questions about the ability and the competence of the City Council to manage and implement urban regeneration. The City Council initially reacted to this by implying there was now a very real possibility that the Estate would be entirely emptied of remaining tenants and the complex returned to the State proper and possibly sold. It was the response of a landlord to an unruly, discommoding tenant. And while the potential of a deliberate and targeted expropriation of the remaining tenants gradually receded, serious issues of trust and good faith remained.

Instead of using the existing Task Force structure, Dublin City Council proposed that an independent facilitator be brought in to convene not just those groups represented at the Task Force, but a wider sector of interests also. When asked what such mediation would achieve the City Council replied that there had been a significant loss of trust in their view and that an independent mediator would help them to reenter the process on terms which they would find acceptable. And yet, even as this concept of mediation was being thrown back and forward, the possibility that the site would be emptied of tenants and closed up or sold was still put forward as a real possibility. If this happened those remaining on the site would be housed elsewhere and the entire regeneration project with all of its aspirations would disappear. The future use of the land would remain uncertain. The Council would fulfill its minimal obligations to rehouse tenants and beyond that nothing else. Its grander, more holistic vision of regeneration would go unfulfilled.

And yet, in tandem with this, a pragmatic, rational approach remained. Selling the site and rehousing tenants would not go unopposed and could potentially generate more overt political action. A negotiated settlement around tenure, densities, heights and community facilities within which the Council could fulfill its own prerequisites was still the best possible outcome for the Council. Officials therefore sought a middle ground that could be found where all parties could find agreement. In response to the idea of mediation, tenants and members of the Regeneration Team suggested that any independent facilitator needed to be briefed. The City Council rejected this suggestion and without forewarning, changed its position on bringing in an independent mediator and moved somewhat suddenly and abruptly to direct negotiations. The two poles that would set the parameters for the negotiations would be the recently rejected City Council Framework Plan and the community plan 'Moving Ahead' which had been rejected by the Department of Environment in 2003. The community plan had contained 320 housing units and a number of community facilities, while the recent Framework Plan developed by the city council had contained in the region of 850 housing units. According to council officials, neither of these positions was acceptable to the other side, there needed to be some way of finding a new position between both which was agreeable to all parties.

In order to bridge the chasm between the two positions it was agreed at the Task Force that two new sub-groups would be set up. They were given crude terms of reference at the outset. One sub-group would work on exploring and initiating a new structure for mediating relations between the various groups involved in regeneration and it was envisaged that this structure would replace the existing Task Force. (This eventually became the St. Michael's Estate Regeneration Board). The other, the work of

Plan A: Moving Ahead

Launched by Dublin City Council in June 2001

After the initial first phase of the regeneration in which 101 social housing units were built on two adjacent sites, the Moving Ahead plan outlined proposals for the provision of 320 units on the original site of St. Michael's Estate. The emphasis in the plan was on the provision of high quality, attractive housing, with a mix of styles and ownership.

The plan included
- Demolition of all existing flats
- 320 housing units overall
- 180 units of social housing
- 70 affordable housing units
- 70 private housing units
- Accommodation for all existing and additional community facilities and services
- Additional childcare provision

This plan was wholeheartedly endorsed by all the stakeholders on the St. Michael's Estate Taskforce and especially by the residents of the estate. It went forward for planning permission in the Summer of 2003, but was rejected by the Department of the Environment who recommended that a Public Private Partnership be pursued instead.

2001

Plan B:
St. Michael's Estate Framework Plan

Launched in 2004
by Dublin City Council

The plan included
Demolition of the existing flats
A sustainable social mix
A sustainable density of c. 60
units to the acre
550 private apartments
80 social housing units
A total of 850 dwellings
Accommodation for all existing
and additional community
facilities and services.

This plan was developed
between Dublin City Council
and a team of architects with
no input or participation from
any of the other parties to
the regeneration process in
St. Michael's Estate. The plan
was put out for 'consultation'
in the summer of 2004. After
a concerted community
campaign this plan was
rejected by the council chamber
of Dublin City Council in
September 2004.

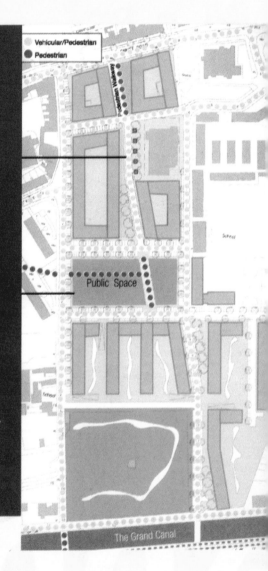

Vehicular/Pedestrian
Pedestrian

Public Space

The Grand Canal

Plan C: The PPP regeneration plan for St. Michael's Estate.

This plan is the winning bid from the PPP competition for St. Michael's Estate. The company McNamara/Castlethorn was chosen from a group o of four bids as the 'Preferred Bidder' for the regeneration of the estate. The plan encompasses 14 acres of land which include a 3 acre site adjacent to Emmet Road that was not originally part of the estate.

Total number of dwellings	720
Total social dwellings	165
Total affordable dwellings	75
Total private dwellings	480

Community Facilities provided
Civic Centre with library
Parish Centre
3 Creches
Youth Centre
Family Resource Centre
Cafes and Restaurants
Supermarket
Primary Health Care Centre
(now on adjoining site)
Guaranteed Fund for Social
Regeneration (Community Safety
and Security, Employment,
Health, Education, Arts and
Culture, Childcare, Sports and
Leisure).

This plan was chosen by the assessment panel which was set up as part of the PPP process. The plan was then given a formal endorsement by the St. Michael's Estate Regeneration Board in 2007. The Project Agreement for the plan is to be officially signed between the developer, McNamara/Castlethorn and Dublin City Council in 2008.

St. Michael's Estate
regeneration

St. Michael's Estate, early 1990s.

The Campaign

The campaign group was set up in April 2004 by the St. Michael's Estate Regeneration Team in response to the rejection by the Department of the Environment to Plan A 'St Michael's Moving Ahead'.

After the official launch in St. Michael's Estate the campaign moved to the steps of Dublin City Council headquarters.

Saint Michael's Estate Community Regeneration Team and Local Residents

John Bissett, author, Nikki Fahey, resident, Caroline Mc Nulty, resident, Rita Fagan, Director of the Family Resource Centre, Helena Burbidge, resident, Ann Marie Brennan, resident, Celine Martin, Team leader Inchicore Community Drug Team, Eilish Comerford, Community Worker Family Resource Centre, Gerry Mc Dermott, St. Michael's Parish Youth Project, Rose Martin, resident, Sr. Jo Kennedy, resident, Michael O Flanagan, resident from Emmet Road.

Missing from the above photo are -

Tasha Farrell, Resident

Sr. Mary-Ann Stafford, Resident

Demolition

July/September 2004
This marks the first of the demolition phase when Blocks 2 and 8 were demolished in conjunction with 1, 3 and 4 of the Senior Citizen Blocks.

This is the land where Blocks 1, 2 and 3 stood. The blocks were demolished in 2004 and there were great expectations that things were moving towards development. The land has been lying idle since, waiting for agreement on a new plan using the PPP model.

Where next?

Bloomsday Protest at Civic Offices 16th June 2008.

which is the subject of this chapter, would attempt to reach agreements on the physical aspects of regeneration of the Estate. Such agreements would encompass the overall number of housing units that would go on the site, the breakdown of these units by housing tenure (social, affordable, private), acceptable heights and densities for the development, the amount of public open space and the amount and type of community and social facilities, initially in square metres, on the site. The agreements reached as part of these negotiations, according to the City Council, would form the basis of a 'brief' that would then be given out to developers.

Prospective bidders would respond to such a brief with 'expressions of interest' and eventually those short listed would submit detailed bids. At the first meeting of this sub-group the Chair of the Task Force clarified the task ahead; 'we are here to negotiate the regeneration of St. Michael's Estate. This falls between the two plans of the recent past. The first part of this takes in the housing content and includes density, heights and the allocation of units between social, private and affordable. The second part is about community services and facilities'. At this stage a cynicism had emerged which overshadowed earlier optimism. St. Michael's Estate was now embarking on its third attempt to negotiate a regeneration agreement. It had proved difficult in the past. At the opening meeting of the negotiations the Chairperson of the Task Force stated strongly that positions should be up front and clear:

> As a model of negotiation I would argue that we put all our cards on the table now. It is in our interests to ensure that everyone puts their full position on the table now and that we then see how everyone can get the most out of their positions. This is not about opening gambits but about bottom lines (Chairperson, St. Michael's Estate Task Force, 10 November, 2004).

The negotiations took place between representative groups and organisations, all of whom were represented on the St. Michael's Estate Task Force. They encompassed Dublin City Council, the St. Michael's Estate Blocks' Committee, the Community Regeneration Team, Connolly Avenue Residents Association and local City Councillors present on the Task Force. In the end there were three formally articulated positions put forward. The first of these was from a local City Councillor, the second from Dublin City Council and the last from the Community Regeneration Team on behalf of the Blocks' Committee on the Estate. The stated position of the Dublin City Councillor was that the estate should contain no more than 500 housing units on the site. Of these between 80 and 100 units should be given over to social housing, and a small percentage of these should be used to house families from the adjacent estate of Tyrone Place. The councillor argued that there would be between 250 and 300 apartments in buildings between three and five storeys in height and that there be a limit of two storeys in any new buildings facing on to Emmet Road.

The original complex of St. Michael's Estate stood on a land bank of eleven acres. The councillor's position above was put forward on the understanding that this was the land that was being negotiated. However, in the recent City Council framework plan that had been rejected, the City Council had incorporated a three acre site on Emmet Road that adjoined the eleven acres. This had been possible because the three acre site contained primarily City Council tenants and other state facilities. At the outset the negotiations took place within the context of the original 11 acres of land. However, as things progressed the other three acres came into play. Potentially therefore, the site could be larger and it also allowed for the possibility that there would be a formal public frontage directly on to the main thoroughfare through Inchicore, Emmet Road. It was within this context that Dublin City Council presented its position on St. Michael's Estate.

Officials argued that the original Community Plan had 320 housing units on 11 acres and that the new Framework Plan had envisaged 850 housing units on 14 acres, of which 625 were on the original 11 acre site. The City Council was prepared to decrease its density from 625 to 500 on the 11 acres. 75 of these units would be social housing units and there would be as much affordable as possible. These would be primarily apartments with a small amount of duplexes and conventional houses. The City Council would try and include some super-affordable housing units at very low cost. The balance of the estate would be private. Within this the council would try and ensure that they would be bought by first time buyers as opposed to investors and speculators. On the question of heights the council did not see anything which would eclipse the current eight storey blocks on the estate. If there was agreement on the densities there could be flexibility on on the heights. The entire development would come out of PPP. Fatima Mansions was used an example of the model where the developer was giving 150 social housing units plus 70 affordable housing units and community facilities as part of the package. In St. Michael's Estate there would be thirty five conventional houses. Officials were adamant that due to new planning requirements, conventional two or three storey housing was almost a thing of the past.

The Council's position encapsulates in microcosm, many of the aspects of a changing City Council philosophy. Increases in the densities of housing units per acre of land, like so many other parts of the city, is a core objective. So too is changing the social structure from being a wholly publicly owned estate to one that will be primarily private. A substantial section of the land will leave City Council ownership and transfer to the private sector. Implicit within all of this is the view that the State will not invest directly in the regeneration of St. Michael's Estate but will instead use its land as a leverage tool. A developer will be given a substantial portion of land in return for building a set amount of housing and facilities. The development is entirely dependent on it being structured and financed through the mechanism of PPP. The example given of Fatima Mansions neglects one important facet of the PPP model: what the State owns before PPP and what it owns after are two different things. The entire infrastructure of social housing and community facilities is to be wholly financed by the estimates of profit to be realised through the sale of private apartments.

Neither the City Councillor nor the City Council gave social housing any real priority in their presentations. In contrast, the retention of social housing had been residents' core priority when they agreed to demolition in 1998. When residents were asked about their wishes for the future of the Estate in 1998:

> ...almost all suggested that the site should be used for local authority housing. No significant indicator arose as to respondents' wish that the site should either be sold off to a private developer for the building of private housing, or that it should continue to be used to provide anything other than houses for the people already living on the Estate who expressed a wish to stay. [51]

And even while the numbers of flats occupied on St. Michael's Estate gradually diminished over the years this remained the central issue from a community perspective. In the first phase of regeneration 101 social housing units had been built on two separate sites adjacent to the Estate for families and older people to move into. The debate was now taking place as to the numbers of social housing that would be guaranteed in this much larger, second phase. In the community plan that had been rejected there had been 170 social housing units as part of a plan with a total of 320 units overall. At the heart of the community strategy on St. Michael's Estate was the belief that social housing should be a substantial and significant aspect of the development. At the second negotiations session, Eilish Comerford, a community worker with the residents on the Estate and a member of the Community Regeneration Team presented a community position and rationale:

> The Council's framework plan is their baseline. This plan [placing a coloured copy of the 'Moving Ahead' community plan on the table] was always our baseline as a starting point. This Community Plan was negotiated over a protracted period of time. The understanding in 1998 in Catherine Morley's document was that all of the tenancies on the Estate would be replaced, all 346 of them. In O'Devaney Gardens the present

position is that for the 276 tenancies [flats] that are currently on the site there is an agreement that they would all be replaced. If the current awareness and knowledge had existed in St. Michael's in 1998 the 346 flats would have been ring fenced and guaranteed to be replaced. There is always a strong sense of grievance about this within St. Michael's Estate. Even within the negotiations over the Community Plan there was a sense then that the community was giving up a lot even then. The land we are talking about is public land and it was a long-held conviction of ours that a substantial proportion of it be used to house people who didn't have access to the private housing market. There are families in Tyrone Place (adjacent social housing flat complex) and there are young people locally who have little or no hope of accessing the housing market. There is also the wider issue of the housing list and of the growing numbers who cannot get access to the housing market. It was our belief that for these reasons there should be a substantial proportion of social housing on the site. Our view is one of social and physical regeneration. We hold an integrated position (November, 2004).

Eilish continued by responding to the City Council's position at the previous meeting and then moved on to the question of the housing tenure mix of any new estate. She presented a revised community position which allowed some room to manoeuvre on the issue of density but which held firmly to the absolute importance of the provision of social housing as the cornerstone of any agreement. These revised estimations were based principally on the retention of a significant social housing stock while giving some leeway on increasing the overall housing densities on the site.

'Moving Ahead' Plan	New Community Proposal
320 housing units overall	450 housing units overall
170 social	225 social
80 affordable	115 affordable
70 private	110 private

The figures in the left hand column were those from the original 'Moving Ahead' plan which had been rejected by the Department of the Environment in 2003. They were a reminder of what had been agreed at that time in principle. The new set of figures on the right was a new community negotiating position. This facilitated an increase in the overall numbers that would go on the site but stayed with the principle of a substantial amount of social housing. The overall density of the Estate would increase to 450 housing units. The City Council queried who was asking for all of this social housing. The Chair reiterated that this had long been a substantive issue. Changing its position, the City Council increased its offer on the numbers of social housing from 75 to 125 but the overall density would have to increase from 500 to 550 on the 11 acres. Given how little movement here had been on social housing this surprised people around the table.

Knowing that the numbers of social housing in their proposal were still someway short of community expectations the City Council made its final offer. The council would go to 150 on the social housing if the affordable was reduced down to 70 and the overall density increased to 575. For every extra public housing unit given there had to be, in the City Council's view, a corresponding private unit in the opposite direction. St. Michael's Estate would get the bulk of its social housing from the rejected plan but the *quid pro quo* was the loss of a substantial section of public land which would be used to build a large number of private housing units. The offer was put but nothing was agreed. Leaving the local community centre that night, there was an initial euphoria at the idea that the City Council were prepared to go back to something close to the number of social housing units that were in the original plan which was rejected. There was a sense of elation and jubilation. The community's core demand had come close to being met. In the Family Resource Centre a mini-celebration ensued.

The issue of social housing had been central to the entire campaign in St. Michael's Estate and there was a feeling that the whole thing was close to a resolution. After the initial elation of achieving close to the core objective on social housing, a period of sober reflection took place within which a deep assessment of what was being offered took place. This culminated with a pre-pared statement by the Community Regeneration Team which was put to the Task Force sub-group and the City Council in particular:

> We have gone back and talked to the residents and groups and community organisations and listened to the sentiments from these sessions. Our first point is that people are generally happy with the social housing and that the offer has been increased to 150 and some of the ideas around the affordable and super affordable and the commitment to build 30 new conventional houses for residents and some of the ideas around mixed housing types. However, serious reservations have been expressed in relation to the enormous number of private apart-ments that have been proposed and that have to go on site for the social housing and community facilities to be delivered. People were genuinely upset and alarmed that their housing is dependent on these huge numbers of private housing going on the site (Eilish Comerford, St. Michael's Estate Community Regeneration Team, 1 December 2004).

A meeting of tenant community groups and Dublin City Coun-cillors was held to debate the merits of the City Council's new proposal. The dilemma of getting local residents housed urgently was to the fore, but those present were clearly aware of the im-plications of doing this using the PPP model.

THE BONES OF A NEW PLAN

The principal elements of the proposal were that the eleven acre site on which St. Michael's Estate originally stood would, after PPP, contain 150 units of social housing, 70 affordable and 355 private units. When added to the 101 social housing units which had been built in the first phase, this proposal would result in the replacement of a substantial bulk of the public housing that had originally been located on the site. It was agreed that negotiations for the community facilities would take place at a later date During the course of the negotiations the three acre site that fronted on to Emmet Road (and not part of the original St. Michael's Estate) formally became part of the regeneration plan. City Council officials were adamant that all of the apartments that would go on this section would be wholly private. Over a period of time and due to intense community pressure, it was agreed that the same ratios would apply to the mixture of social/affordable and private on this three acres as did to the original 11 acre site of St. Michael's Estate.

In retrospect, St. Michael's Estate could have attempted to campaign politically to defeat the overarching mechanism of Public Private Partnership and advocate a State-funded programme of regeneration. For many reasons, however, paramount of which was the urgent need to provide housing for those still living on the Estate and to retain as many of the remaining tenants as possible, the proposal was accepted. A number of conditions were put together and written up that would be lodged as part of the community position on the proposal. Chief among these was the declaration that the agreement that had been reached through the negotiations on the tenure mix of the new estate would not forthwith be changed by any other party. This was consolidated by others which included the making of a strong case for intense community participation in the design of any new plan, that the State invest in the regeneration of the Estate, and that a process begin soon to craft much needed community facilities. These conditions were read into the minutes of the sub group after the following short preamble:

> We are aware that in most negotiations compromise is essential if the core issues are to be resolved and differences reconciled. We feel that we have compromised hugely during this process. Within these negotiations there have been and

continue to be issues and practices that we pointedly disagree with. We have made these well known during the course of these current series of meetings. However, as we have always done, we acknowledge the urgency of the issues facing the residents of St. Michael's Estate and the need to restart the regeneration process quickly. We have decided that the negotiated settlement that is currently on the table for the new St. Michaels Estate is agreeable to but under strict conditions (Eilish Comerford, St. Michael's Estate Task Force, 13 December 2004).

SUMMARY

Looking back over the negotiations, it is clear that there was more than one 'regeneration' going on. There were two diametrically opposed views as to the best way forward for the regeneration of the Estate. There were clear differences as to how regeneration would happen in St. Michael's Estate. Such differences manifested themselves most lucidly around the provision and status of social housing. Within the negotiations social housing became something of a marginalised category. From a community perspective the necessity of providing social housing was defended fiercely. Against this, Dublin City Council built all of its negotiation strategies and tactics around privatising the Estate using the logic of 'the market'. Within the mechanism of PPP the provision of social housing was entirely dependent on the sale of private apartments. From such a market perspective, it made perfectly logical sense to shrink and minimise the social housing sector on the Estate. On many occasions, the provision of social housing was referred to as something that was making the overall regeneration project "marginal". This is summed up in a phrase used by officials at more than one meeting, "Because there is significant social housing it leaves very little in the pot". It strikes one as not a little strange that the City Council, which has a clear responsibility to provide housing for those who cannot access the private market, was itself driving such a process.

Chapter 8

'Tenants First':
A Solidarity Narrative

...one day in the Spring of 1973, like the dinosaurs, they suddenly disappeared. Their trace, to be precise, still remains on the Parisian soil; the buildings are there, the people are there, and the housing bureaucracy is there. But these are remnants. From Spring 1973 on, not a single Grand Ensemble was to be built. Nor were they to be replaced as they decayed. And as with the dinosaurs, it was a sudden extinction that remains at first sight, a mystery.[52]

C hapter 3 set St. Michael's Estate within the wider policy context of regeneration in the city over the past twenty years. However, in recent years Dublin has witnessed the embryonic beginnings of community responses to such policies. The purpose of this chapter is to place St. Michael's Estate within this broader, citywide frame of grassroots responses to such structural change. In particular this chapter will focus on the attempt by communities to develop a citywide organisation which could respond in some way to the State's regeneration programme. St. Michael's Estate is but one small piece of an overall regeneration jigsaw for state owned housing complexes in Dublin city. And, just like the 'Grand Ensembles' or large suburban housing estates of Paris that Manuel Castells describes above, many are in the process of disappearing from the landscape completely. The list of complexes and estates proposed for regeneration has grown longer and longer in recent years. As well as St. Michael's Estate, O'Devaney Gardens, Fatima Mansions, Dominic Street, Chamber Court, Dolphin House, St. Teresa's Gardens, and Charlemount Street are just some of the others that have been ring fenced for regeneration. (Almost all of these complexes are for total demolition, and almost all are designated to be regenerated using Public Private Partnership). Regeneration therefore, is not an isolated issue for a small number of residents in a single complex, but instead is taking on the shape of a more general social process in the city at large.

Initially, individual complexes responded to the overtures of the State based on local understanding and need. The nature of such responses has varied enormously across the city and has been closely related to the resources, power and capacity of local communities to articulate a position or set of clearly defined needs. One of the characteristics of regeneration at a community level has been its individualised and particular nature. For a period of time, estates and complexes knew little of what was happening in the rest of the city and there was little for them to benchmark their own experience against. Knowledge of the broader regeneration context remained fragmented and incomplete and was dispersed in bits and pieces throughout the city. Perhaps the only place such an overview was held in its totality was on a wall chart in Dublin City Council. A community-based, holistic comprehension of regeneration at this broader level was still a long way off. For a period of time, local complexes and estates were largely unaware of the commonality of the regeneration processes taking place across the city.

However, given the proposed scale of such change, flat complexes and estates began to seek each other out and to share regeneration experiences and stories. One of the tentative steps in this direction began with dialogues between O'Devaney Gardens, Fatima Mansions and St. Michael's Estate about the respective processes in each of the estates, all three of which are located within relatively short distances of each other. These early meetings took the form of sharing stories on the regeneration experiences across the three council estates. These dialogues were particularly insightful in understanding the motivation and objectives of the State in each complex and, toward the end of 2003, these conversations filtered out into other complexes in the metropolitan area. The idea of bringing together as many complexes as possible in the city began to take shape. The simple goal was to explore the possibilities of a broader collective understanding of regeneration.

A COLLECTIVE UNDERSTANDING OF THE CHANGING CITY

The first attempt at bringing a broad group of communities together took place in November 2003 in the refurbished City Council flat complex of Killarney Court, formerly St. Joseph's Mansions, in Dublin's north inner city, and was facilitated by Community Technical Aid.[53] A number of flat complexes, estates and community groups and organisations were invited to this meeting to discuss the 'the future direction of social housing in Dublin City and the potential effect of Public Private Partnerships on public housing and inner city communities'. For many of those present this was ostensibly a first collective attempt at trying untangle the State's changing relationship to publicly owned complexes and estates. It was also a first attempt at trying to explain where things were at and why. Residents were given basic information on the policies coming on stream which would affect both current and future generations of tenants. Residents listened as the various strategies and options being sought by the City Council were outlined. These included the sale of City Council flats to tenants (also known as the 'Right to Buy'), the use of Public Private Partnership in regeneration, the deterioration of maintenance in many of the City Council's flat complexes, and finally, the arrangements for the provision and management of social housing in the city in the future. Beneath all of these initiatives was the changing role and function of the City Council in relation to social housing. Whether Dublin City Council would continue to act as landlord to its tenants was uncertain. There were clear indications that the management and organisation of social housing in the city was undergoing a reorientation. The clearest evidence that such a process was underway were given by many of those present.

Residents from various complexes on the night began to tell their own regeneration stories. Those from St. Michael's Estate, O'Devaney Garden's, Fatima Mansions and Cork Street/ Coombe amongst others, brought people up to speed on what was happening on the ground. There was a cross referencing of experience from place to place. This was the first occasion when communities began to place themselves within the context of a city wide landscape. Many of those present on the night described estates in various shades of deterioration and dilapidation where there had been little or no investment in the physical or social infrastructure for many years. It was usually within such a context that the City Council was arriving with proposals for redevelopment. The timing of regeneration was important in that it seemed to happen when many communities were at their lowest point. Officials argued that this provided a perfect justification for regeneration. In many Dublin City housing estates and flat complexes the option being strongly proposed by officials was that of Public Private Partnership. In practice this meant proposing significant numbers of private housing units on what were previously wholly owned and run City Council estates. Where possible, social housing was to be correspondingly reduced. Many complexes had great difficulty understanding what was proposed and how it would happen. In many of the communities present, there was a lack of organisational structures to enable response to such proposals. The issues of capacity, skills and resources were clearly apparent. Some estates had longer development histories than others and had built up capacity and skills pools over a considerable period of time. Others who were working from a completely voluntary basis were encountering this process for the first time. These capacity issues were producing significant variations in community responses to regeneration at local level. Many groups expressed dismay at the speed at which such changes were expected to happen.

As the meeting progressed it also became clear that communities were at different stages on their respective regeneration journeys. Some were scratching the surface of possibilities while others were in the midst of tendering for master plans. The various stories revealed the 'manysidedness' of the process from the political, to the economic, to the social and to the architectural/technical. At this stage communities had drawn little differentiation between these various layers and tended not to disaggregate the component parts of the process. Pointed questions were asked as to what options communities really did have. How would they define what was important to them? If they didn't like what was happening could they stop it? The overwhelming sense from the meeting was of an accelerated process of change happening in many areas of the city. What was being proposed in many of the complexes was complete demolition and rebuild from scratch. More often than not this appeared to involve a marginalisation of the social housing sector. The meeting was a first attempt at trying to come to terms with and to understand such change on a collective basis.

ESTABLISHING AND SUSTAINING A GRASSROOTS TENANTS ORGANISATION

The nature of the change for complexes across the city posed many questions not least of which was how to respond. What problems were there with the changes which were taking place? Was it possible to come up with a unified position around such changes and to challenge the State if necessary? What were the needs of communities in relation to such changes and how could they be supported? How would complexes and estates organise themselves? On the back of this meeting in Killarney Court a small sub-group was established to draw up initial terms of reference for a new grassroots organisation. A discussion from the first meeting of this sub-group encapsulates this attempt at trying to make sense of the whole process:

> Mick: People in traditional flat complexes are now faced with the land being taken away. What have we got in common? Are we a group or an alliance of groups?
>
> Charlie: We're all under the threat of the privatisation of social housing.
>
> Joe: This is a forum of community organisations based in local authority flat complexes/estates.
>
> Patricia: Isn't it about the sale of public land, or the transfer of land?
>
> Lena: I have no idea of our rights as tenants. They can't sell the land with tenants on it.
>
> Mick: Is that true? They detenanted Sheriff Street and then privatised the land.
>
> Patricia: It's a constitutional issue.
>
> Mick: Is this group about a single issue focus? We need to research the different stages that community groups are at.
>
> Charlie: The focus should be on one complex.
>
> Patricia: The emphasis on social housing is always on the negative. There is a positive history of social housing from the beginning of the State (Family Resource Centre, St. Michael's Estate, 25 November 2003).

It was clear that the State was well organised and resourced to pursue its regeneration objectives. It also had a new energy and sense of purpose with its mission. Some of this undoubtedly had to do with taking on an 'entrepreneurial' development role within the city. But how would communities organise themselves? Large meetings could be called, but could a commonly articulated understanding develop? Gradually, from these large public meetings, a loose organisational structure took shape. The name 'Tenants First' was put forward and subsequently adopted to give a sense of identity to the organisation. At a public meeting in Francis Street in February, 2004, draft terms of reference were put out for testing and clarification with a number of complexes in the city. Tenants First defined itself as a "non-party political, non-sectarian forum," where "individual group members were free to act autonomously at all times". One of the key aims of this new organisation would be "to respond collectively to the policy changes which will lead to an overall reduction in public housing by Dublin City Council". The membership of the organisation was open to "local authority tenants in the Dublin area and to community/support groups working with them".

The fledging organisation described itself as a "forum of local authority community organisations" with one of its primary functions "to share information and to provide support to each other". One observation made within the terms of reference highlighted "the deliberate running down of flat complexes by Dublin City Council resulting in the "break up of working class communities making it impossible to sustain community infrastructure". Another read "it is a question of land use and of social as opposed to capitalist values". All of this was refined and a formal terms of reference was presented to a meeting of complexes and estates from all over the city in Killarney Court in February 2004.

> Tenants First's aim is to provide a strong collective voice for local tenants on issues and concerns that residents and their local representatives are experiencing concerning their living and housing conditions.
>
> Tenants First is a forum of tenants representatives from the wider Dublin area who have come together to share information, experiences and support each other around issues of common concern (Tenants First, Organisational Terms of Reference, February 2004).

Responding to the establishment of this new organisation, tenants and organisations raised a number of issues. When the terms of reference were presented, a central concern was the participation of tenants in any new organisational structure. It was argued that "the proposed structure is excellent but how do local tenants fit into it, we must get tenants themselves directly involved". The whole issue of capacity was recognised as being central to such a challenge. "Tenants First needs to build in areas where groups are weak, we need to build up our organisational capacity". There was an awareness that understanding the larger framework within which all of this change was taking place, was still a critical task. Residents clearly identified the City Council as the primary force in all of this. It was acknowledged that complexes and estates would continue to work on their respective projects at local level. At this initial stage communities' needs were rooted in trying to understand what was happening. There was a huge need for information and knowledge about what was being proposed.

Even at this early stage, the difference between local community strategies and the development of a broader, political position on housing posed a dilemma. This question as to whether a broader set of political objectives could be determined while flat complexes and estates continued to negotiate locally was one that was to continue for some time. Much of the early work in Tenants First was given over to facilitating communities to express core issues of concern. Public meetings were held on an almost monthly basis with such intentions in mind. Simultaneously, communities were coming together and an organisational structure was growing and developing. This needed to happen in a way that communities could understand and participate in. It needed an appropriate process that could provide a counterpoint to the experience of alienation that many complexes were experiencing.

ENTERING THE LARGER POLITICAL DEBATE ON HOUSING

Tenants First had come into being as a result of the changing housing policy context in the city of Dublin. In September 2003, at the same time as the formal announcement of the rejection of the 'Moving Ahead' plan in St. Michael's Estate, the City Council distributed a position paper entitled *Discussion report on the possible transfer of ownership of City Council rented housing stock*.[54] In this brief seven page document, Dublin City Council set out the case for changes within the ownership, management and maintenance of its own housing stock. The paper encapsulated, in microcosm, a City Council redefining its relationship to social housing. The City Council argued that social housing, while necessary, did not have to be provided directly by the council. The City Council also proposed that the numbers of units managed by them could be reduced and management functions transferred to other housing associations and companies. The City Council was of the view that "having a greater range of landlords could help eliminate the stigma attached to social housing". Ultimately such a policy shift "would allow us (the City Council) to manage a lesser stock of dwellings and allow us to concentrate on more proactive and strategic issues surrounding housing in the city".[55] The landlord/tenant relationship was at the core of the entire discussion paper which made it abundantly clear that the City Council would like much less of landlord role and to divest itself of most if not all such responsibility. Housing associations and possibly even tenant associations could take up this role into the future. Killarney Court, an old City Council complex in the heart of the north inner city was given as an example. The Estate is now run by Cluaid Housing Association and is held up as an exemplar of such new forms of management where the council is not involved.

It was within this changing policy context that Tenants First was invited to City Hall in Dublin to address the Strategic Policy Committee on Housing (SPCH) of Dublin City Council in March

2004. The meeting took place in the Council Chamber. Many local Councillors were present as was the Assistant City Manager for Housing. As part of a collective Tenants First presentation, residents from Cork Street, O'Devaney Gardens, St. Michael's Estate and Fatima Mansions addressed the Council. Tenants First posed specific questions about the proposals for the transfer of ownership of publicly-owned flats and the use of Public Private Partnership in the regeneration of publicly-owned estates and complexes. In particular the questions focused on the financial rationale behind PPP, the safeguarding of tenants' rights, and the net loss of social housing units in the city. More general questions were also posed as to the level of resident participation, knowledge and control over such changes. Would residents have an input or a say in these critical decisions? The current lack of information and consultation on the proposed changes at local level was highlighted, as was the long term future of social housing in the city. And while the City Councillors present thanked Tenants First for a thought-provoking presentation, the questions posed, for the most part, remained unanswered. Those representing Tenants First were left with the impression that the power over and knowledge of the proposed changes lay more with council officials and civil servants than with elected councillors.

The Assistant City Manager for Housing welcomed the Tenants First presentation and remarked that the City Council's paper should be read more as a set of ideas than a concrete proposal. Such a large scale change would take time, and would probably only happen estate by estate. He went on to suggest that the right of city council tenants to buy their own flats was a controversial issue and that there was lots of misleading information floating around in relation to PPPs, which according to him, were merely joint ventures between the council and private developers. From his perspective PPPs were now an opportunity to get redevelopment done.

The encounter in City Hall highlighted the fact that Tenants First was grappling with the proposed changes for social housing across the city. It was the first official encounter between the fledgling organisation and the city's institutions. The encounter was the epitome of decorum and reasonableness and there was no overt confrontation. And yet, neither was there any real, critical engagement across the floor of the Chamber. The engagement was superficial and the rationale behind the proposed changes remained hidden. If Tenants First was hoping for illumination, the questions asked elicited little by the way of substantive response. There was no incremental increase in knowledge about the financial mechanism of PPP, nor on a general blueprint for social housing in the city. As the Assistant City Manager remarked, "all we are doing is bringing forward ideas". Such ideas however were increasingly taking on a life of their own, especially those relating to PPP.

THE REAL GUIDE TO REGENERATION FOR COMMUNITIES

Over time Tenants First began to devote its energies to working at a grassroots level with flat complexes, estates and residents/tenants associations. This was done primarily through the holding of regular public meetings and workshops. Tenants First was attempting to use a community development model of practice where issues were identified from the ground up and were not externally imposed. At a citywide workshop in May 2005, regeneration was identified as a priority theme for Tenants First to work on in the short to medium term. It was suggested that a 'toolbox' document could be valuable to those communities who were facing the prospect of regeneration locally. The simple premise behind the toolbox was to pool the general learning that had accrued in individual estates to date and to synthesise it into one document.

This became the *Real Guide to Regeneration for Communities*, [56] a brief document which functioned on a number of levels. Its most important function was simply to point out to communities that regeneration was a decision that they should be involved in making. The *Real Guide* asked communities to think critically about the process, they were about to embark upon. Building on knowledge gained from estates already engaged in the process it provided a realistic appraisal as to what would actually happen once regeneration was underway. Higher densities, substantial numbers of additional private units, loss of public open space and the loss of neighbours and community were inevitable side effects of regeneration. The community left at the end of the process often bore little resemblance to that at the outset. The State's advances to local communities presented the case for regeneration as inevitable and irresistible and wholly positive. And while there were undoubted benefits to regeneration, the *Real Guide* asked communities to consider and evaluate the effects and outcomes of this process prior to making a decision. It was not by necessity a *fait accompli* that regeneration was inevitable. Communities had the right to "make a democratic decision, for depopulation, demolition or redevelopment", but they also had the right to "keep the Estate and the community together and retain the existing space".[57]

The *Real Guide* also recognised the harsh and sometimes intolerable realities for communities on the ground. The material conditions in many estates made a proposal for regeneration difficult if not impossible to resist. A number of the older complexes in the city were already engaged in PPP projects within their own estates. And yet communities involved in regeneration through PPP had identified a number of ongoing issues once a decision had been made. How would the social-private housing ratio be decided? What sort of community facilities would be provided? Would there be investment in the social regeneration of estates? PPP was an intensely technical process and it was quite easy for communities to get lost along the way. One of the lessons from communities engaged in PPP was the importance of developing and having access to a broad range of skills and capacities. The scale of these new projects placed many estates and community development organisations in completely new territory. Communities needed more than just community development skills for such a process. One of the areas that came increasingly to the fore was that of the architectural and planning supports that communities needed to understand and participate in PPP. Another was the establishment of properly resourced structures within which relationships between all of the relevant parties could be managed and mediated.

The *Real Guide* therefore attempted to reshape the debate on the regeneration of social housing estates by arguing that communities could actually say no or yes to what was on offer. Prior to this the debate was framed in such a way that regeneration was a decision that had already been taken and that it was really about negotiating local agreements within this framework thereafter. The *Real Guide* posed the question, could communities begin to take some control over these processes and act for themselves? The Real Guide was launched in April, 2006 and subsequently used as a practical tool in workshops.

The *Real Guide* raised many questions, but perhaps some of the most pressing had to do with the relationships between power, leadership and urban regeneration. In order to get to the heart of such issues and continuing its practice of facilitating estates and flat complexes directly, Tenants First held a workshop in October 2006 around these entwined themes.[58] The workshop was to focus principally on community power and leadership within the grassroots itself. But the reality that communities are caught up in wider power structures was brought home very quickly at the beginning of the session. Residents arrived from a City Council flat complex and told of an immediate crisis as the council had arrived out of the blue with draft plans for the future of the Estate and was expecting them to be signed off on quickly. A discussion on an abstract theme suddenly took on an intense immediacy. A number of people present on the day took time out from the agenda and spent the morning assisting this group with their dilemma. The predicament they found themselves in was one that had been happening frequently to complexes around the city. They were caught between the reality of a deteriorating City Council complex and a City Council pressurising local people for instant decisions:

> Gina: Can they say that because this thing isn't signed we can't give you social housing?

> Joe: It's essentially about power and how you negotiate what you are looking for. Unless you get the power structure right. This is the most common denominator. The City Council says 'we'll walk away'. They can do this because of the power structures. Unless the detail is right and the regeneration is negotiated through the structure.

> Danny: The greatest power you have is your feet. You just walk out. Until you get what you want you just tell them to get lost. They are comin' to regenerate us. Until you do this power will remain with them (Tenants First Workshop, October 2006).

This particular crisis highlighted more than any planned workshop could have, the relationship between power and urban regeneration. A small group of those present worked directly with the residents who had arrived to find a workable solution to the current situation. As this took place, other groups explored and analysed the effects of leadership at personal, community and citywide levels. For those local residents who had gotten involved in regeneration, they had done so because the issues 'were very close to their own life and beliefs'. By placing themselves in leadership roles they were taking risks and potentially making themselves vulnerable to criticism not just from the State but also from neighbours, and even friends. They had learned that understanding and managing community politics was a difficult and sensitive task. They were also of the view that the State would much prefer to work with docile and pliable residents who didn't challenge or critique what the State was proposing. Over time however, they had grown in confidence and had become stronger in their views and thinking.

Deirdre: Regeneration has been a challenge. But I have grown more confident at it and giving it back to the City Council. I first got involved through a public meeting in the flats seven years ago. When regeneration started off the Council dealt with you with a wink and a nod. The Council wants residents who won't answer back.

Catherine: It empowers you. You lose your shyness and it gives you more confidence.

Deirdre: When you're on the board you talk back to them and argue with them and disagree with them.

Nora: But its not just us. There's strength in numbers (Tenants First Workshop, October 2006).

It was also acknowledged that from a community perspective, responding to regeneration was a complicated issue:

Eilish: Dublin City Council targets residents with these vague framework plans. And some flat complexes have no infra-structure. You need to have confidence to hold your nerve. The length of time that regeneration takes makes it difficult to hold people. There is always a pressure to make quick decisions (Tenants First Workshop, October 2006).

The practicalities of influencing the City Council and effecting change from a community basis was well recognised.

Joe: How do we, as an organisation, with all of us going back to work in our own organisations, affect policy and practice at a council level? There is something about knowing what the City Council does. How does a woman feel so petrified? Its easy for all of us. But there needs to be something to put pressure on the Council to behave in a particular way.

Mairin: Being a model of good behaviour helps, being transparent and being able to answer the question 'who gave you a mandate?', and being clear about how you are doing it. Yes, you have to be strategic and organised.

Niall: The way I see it Tenants First has pressing choices. Things such as affiliating support, doing case studies. But on the broader level, on a citywide level, things haven't been represented critically on policy or on the behaviour modification of DCC as a dysfunctional organisation. We need to bring it into the public domain. We need discipline, communication and evidence to back it up. It is so bad that at European level they are saying that we are the worst case of urban development in Europe. As a local authority our model is skewed in Dublin. We are in a feudal period (Tenants First Workshop, October 2006).

Tenants First continues to work with flat complexes and estates across the city of Dublin. Other groups from outside the capital have also begun to connect to this process. Given the limited resources available to the organisation, having no staff and minimal funding, it has managed to provide many spaces within which dialogue has begun across the city of Dublin as to the future of publicly-owned housing complexes in the city. One of its most critical functions in recent years has been to create the conditions for solidarity to develop amongst the many complexes experiencing change. It has also begun to critique the State's policies in the city and challenge the dominant orthodoxies in relation to regeneration. This has not been without its contradictions. The right to buy is one such area where individual tenants are seeking to buy their flats from the City Council. However this council strategy raises questions as to the future generations who will need such housing and where, if at all, it will be provided. There is also a, perhaps positive, tension between autonomy at local level and the development of a coherent political position across the city. The experience of Tenants First is that such a development will take time. However, one thing is certain, through workshops, forums and publications such as the *Real Guide* there has been and continues to be an intense debate on such issues across the City Council flat complexes and estates of the city. Perhaps the most noticeable thing to happen has been the gradual increase in the knowledge base of communities on the ground. To use Freire's[59] term, a slow "conscientization" has begun around regeneration and around public-housing issues in general.

Chapter 9

'Doing' PPP

Commodities cannot themselves go to market and perform exchanges in their own right. We must, therefore, have recourse to their guardians, who are the possessors of commodities. Commodities are things, and therefore lack the power to resist man. If they are unwilling, he can use force; in other words, take possession of them...commodities must be realized as values before they are realized as use-values.[60]

Having taken a brief overview of regeneration from a citywide perspective, it is time to return to St. Michael's Estate and the detail of using a Public Private Partnership for the regeneration of the Estate. Once the broad agreements on critical issues such as housing tenure were reached in negotiations on the core content of the PPP, a new phase of the process effectively began. In a somewhat simplified sense, this can be broken down into two distinct components. Firstly, there was the development of a brief that would be given to those developers tendering for the project. In the language of PPP, the brief is known as the 'Request for Proposals' (RFP). The RFP would contain a set of expectations on the design and financing of the project to be met by interested bidders. The second broad element of regeneration to be worked on was the development of a new regeneration structure within which all of the parties to regeneration would come together.

I want to begin with the latter of these, the formal, structural arrangements between all of the relevant parties. The St. Michael's Estate Task Force had fulfilled this function in an *ad hoc* capacity for much of the early history of regeneration from the time demolition was agreed in 1998 right up until 2004. In April 2005, the Task Force was officially disbanded and all members of the Task Force resigned as did the Chair. The new St. Michael's Estate Regeneration Board was formally constituted in 2005 and a new Chair agreed by all of the parties was appointed. Many organisations that had been formerly represented on the Task Force would also be represented on the new Board. Perhaps the critical difference between old and new structures was the fact that the new Board would be allocated resources, premises, staff and administrative support to work on the project full time. (Such resources as well as the City Council Project Team, would ultimately be funded through the PPP). In theory, the Board would function as a forum within which all of the parties to regeneration would agree a common regeneration agenda. It would be made up of local tenants, community groups and organisations working in and around the Estate, officials from state agencies including Dublin City Council and the Gardai, and elected City Councillors.

TAKING THE CHAIR

The establishment of the Regeneration Board was in many ways an attempt to re-establish the regeneration process. Given the recent tumultuous history, it would undoubtedly be a challenge to develop a structure which could successfully mediate the relationships between all of the parties to the process, in particular relations between community and state. The role of Chair would be critical to successfully steering a course for the future St. Michael's Estate. At a first, exploratory meeting in April 2005, the new Chair, Finbarr Flood, expounded the following view on the role and purpose of such a Board:

> We agree what the project is and whatever we arrive at we coordinate all the various skills and bodies to a common purpose. The Board will agree the framework for the bricks

and mortar and the social agenda. It is very positive, we need both but sometimes it is very difficult. One without the other is no good. My job is to drive and focus. You will have preferences for who you represent. When the Board is set up you will have a different role. It doesn't mean you give up your own role. The overall good of the project becomes the priority and it is not an easy role.

With this approach, the Regeneration Board becomes the pivotal funnel through which everything must pass and within which the core energy of regeneration resides. All of the respective parties are asked to put aside their differences and work together as a collective in the pursuit of a singular regeneration agenda. The Board attempts to develop a singular vision and a unilateral sense of purpose. Given the difficulties that had arisen in St. Michael's Estate the management of the various perspectives was going to be a critical task. In practical terms, all detailed work on regeneration was delegated to sub-groups or working-groups of the Board. The Board itself received progress reports from such sub-groups and the Chair placed these within the context of an overall regeneration programme. Modifications were made where necessary or as required. For the new Chair regeneration was, above all, a pragmatic task to be accomplished.

DESIGNING A SCHEME FOR REMAINING RESIDENTS

Setting up new structures was paralleled by continuing work on the physical design of the new Estate. There were still 40 to 50 families left on St. Michael's Estate in desperate need of housing. Most of these had women as the heads of household, and many were single parents. It was usually these women who attended meetings and who were, for many years, the backbone of community involvement in the regeneration. Work had been ongoing to fast track the design of a housing scheme for these remaining tenants on a specific section of the Estate. A four acre site adjacent to the graveyard and the canal towards the back of the site, which had been developed in the original 'Moving Ahead' plan, was reactivated and residents became actively involved in this process. Sketches were drawn up and a new architectural blueprint took shape quite quickly. Whoever was awarded the contract for the new Estate would do so on the condition that this section would be built first with the utmost immediacy. There was a strong sense that these last remaining residents had had it harder than most and that their housing needs should be treated with urgency. Because of this, the four acre site was designed to a high degree of detail. All of the house types, tenure, heights, materials, open space and play areas were clearly defined. Residents could see their new homes being developed in the plans and had acquired an intimate knowledge of this part of the scheme. Even so, residents were still uncertain as to whether they could sustain living on the Estate until new houses were built given the harshness of the conditions.

This design of the housing scheme for the remaining residents was crafted to a high level of detail because of the urgency of their housing needs. The rest of the site (10 acres) would be left to the imagination of architectural teams working for prospective bidders and would form the core content of the PPP competition. Ultimately there would be a holistic plan for the Estate comprising both sections which would cover an area of some fourteen acres. Bidders would be given a set of requirements in the RFP and they, in turn, would submit new master plans for the Estate. As well as outlining the physical and financial requirements of the PPP for St. Michael's Estate, the RFP also detailed the process by which proposals would be evaluated and measured.

THE ASSESSMENT PROCESS FOR PUBLIC PRIVATE PARTNERSHIP

In accordance with the public procurement guidelines for PPP projects, a formal evaluation of the bids would take place according to criteria laid down in the RFP. An 'Evaluation/Assessment Panel' would be set up specifically for this task and would include technical, financial and legal advisers to assess and evaluate bids for the appointment of the 'Preferred Bidder' for the project. ('Preferred Bidder' is the name given to the winning bid.) Residents and community organisations at the Regeneration Board had not encountered such a process before and had little knowledge as to how this would happen in practice. From the State's perspective, the make-up of this panel was unproblematic. It would be made up of 'various professional experts' from various departments of Dublin City Council, including architects, quantity surveyors and valuers. It would also include the Process Auditor from the Department of the Environment, representatives from the National Development Finance Agency (NDFA) and if needed, independent financial expertise would be utilised. However, the panel as proposed, left no space for community expertise and participation. Community representatives at the Board posed questions as to the exclusive nature of the panel. This ignited a dispute that was to run for considerable time. Initial reactions to this highlighted the sensitivity about access to such a space.

City Council officials argued that the community could influence the process locally and should trust the 'professional experts' with making the critical decision on a new masterplan for the Estate. They also maintained that being a participant on the Assessment Panel carried with it potential legal liability and risk to the individual. The intimation was that developers could potentially sue individuals if they were unhappy with the outcome of the panel's deliberations. And while state employees, by their very location, appeared to have a superhero-like protection against any impending lawsuit or legal action, community representatives, at this stage, could not be afforded the same cover. However, the community sector was determined in its belief that participation on the Assessment Panel would be critical to the future of the new Estate. This view was encapsulated in a statement to the Regeneration Board:

...we feel it is imperative that we be represented on the Assessment Panel of the procurement process for a developer for St. Michael's Estate. At its simplest our position is based on the belief that we should be active participants of the process at every level within which the developer is being chosen for the regeneration of St. Michael's Estate. If we were building a house we would want to choose the builder would we not? The Assessment Panel as it is currently set up gives undue weight to planners, architects, officials etc., and has no input or direction from the community sector. We feel that residents and community groups should be part of the assessment process in order to facilitate community input at this phase of the regeneration process (St. Michael's Estate Blocks' Committee Position Paper to the Regeneration Board, 7 July 2005).

The City Council eventually conceded to one person from the Regeneration Board being a participant on the panel. The council was also strongly of the view that this person should preferably have 'planning or technical expertise'. Residents and community groups had argued that two places on the panel should be given over to community participation. After a protracted period of time, a final resolution to this was achieved when the City Council reluctantly agreed to two community members of the Board going forward as members of the Assessment Panel.

The debate over participation on the Assessment Panel had gone on for over a year, but the community's persistence and determination achieved a positive result in the end. The length of time it had taken had shown just how difficult it was to alter a single element of the PPP structure. Perhaps the most critical of the issues raised was the community's right to be part of the decision of choosing a developer and a new masterplan for the Estate. The way the Assessment Panel had originally been constituted would have denied residents and local organisations the right to such a choice. Instead, the choice would have been made by others and delivered locally as a *fait accompli*. The agreement that there would be two places at the Assessment Panel for community representatives from the Regeneration Board was a breaking of new ground. Two community representatives would now be present at the assessment of all of the bids for the new St. Michael's Estate.

WRITING A JOB DESCRIPTION FOR PPP; A REQUEST FOR PROPOSALS

Because the regeneration of St. Michael's Estate was to be done through PPP the entire structuring of the project had different characteristics to a traditional tender. The first part of this process involved an 'Expressions of Interest' advertisement being placed in the *Irish Times* on 30 May 2005. This is also known as a 'Request for Qualifications'(RFQ).This marked the official entry of St. Michael's Estate into the public sphere as a PPP project. The RFQ was a first trawl for interested developers/consortia with the requisite skills, capacity, experience and money to undertake a project of this scale. There was a surge of interest in the development in these initial stages. Within the first week of the advertisement being published in the *Irish Times* a dozen parties had already paid the €200 fee for general information on the development. Initially, there were some twenty five expressions of interest in the development in St. Michael's Estate.

Over time, however, it became clear that there were only a handful of developers/consortia who possessed all of the necessary capacities to take on a project of this scale. Many of those who had sought information on the proposed project did not retain their interest. In the end a small group of four developers/consortia were short-listed for the project. Each of these was given a copy of the detailed 'Request for Proposals' (RFP). The core elements of the RFP were the agreements reached between the community and the City Council as part of the recent protracted negotiations around social, affordable and private housing, community and commercial facilities, public open space and agreed heights for the development. The RFP was effectively a

job specification for the regeneration of St. Michael's Estate and
set out Dublin City Council's requirements in terms of technical,
performance, contractual and procedural requirements for the
procurement process of PPP. The RFP outlined the conditions
under which Dublin City Council would enter into an arrangement whereby the private partner would design, build and finance
the social and affordable housing and civic/community elements
of the project in exchange for being granted the development
rights to a specific amount of commercial development space and
to a specific number of private residential accommodation units.
In general, all of the material presented in the RFP can be brought
together under the general headings of finance and design. There
were two printed documents to the RFP, one set out the financial
requirements for the bid, while the other set out what was required in design terms. The two categories were both given overall weighted values which would then be used as measurement
indicators when the bids were being assessed. The weightings for
the PPP in St. Michael's Estate were as follows

- Finance 50 per cent
- Design 45 per cent
- Timescale 5 per cent

On the financial side of the PPP, the RFP stipulated that, to be
compliant, all bidders had to clearly indicate in their completed
financial model the nature of any 'cash offer' (in addition to the
provision of 165 social units and civic/community facilities) they
were prepared to offer Dublin City Council in consideration for
being awarded the project, or if they thought they could not do
this, they should indicate the subsidy they required from the
City Council to provide the 165 social units and community facilities and the other requirements outlined in the RFP and final
contract.

Understandably, the design aspect of the project was extremely important to residents and community representatives.
There were disagreements as to how much design detail should be

included in the RFP. The City Council argued that less was more and that developers should be given flexibility and latitude in their development of a master plan. By contrast at community-based meetings, there was intense debate and discussion on design issues. Residents and community groups worked closely with an experienced architect and in the end there was a strong belief that the more detail in the RFP the better it would be for current and future residents of the Estate. The instructions given out in the RFP would have clear effects not just on what could be built but also on the quality of the new housing and facilities. This came right down to the numbers of sockets in rooms, the materials used in windows, the energy efficiency ratings of the housing units etc. There was a fear that if all of these things weren't indicated clearly then developers would invariably take the cheapest option.

CHOOSING A NEW PLAN FOR ST. MICHAEL'S ESTATE

In the end, the design element of the RFP was developed to quite a high level of detail and it subsequently went out to the respective developers. They in turn responded with their proposed plans for the Estate. On 31 October 2006, the Assessment Panel met for the first time in a windowless room in the bowels of Dublin City Council's offices on Wood Quay. This was the first official engagement of the Panel and the meeting was heavily laden with formality. Seated around a large board table, a number of State officials were present from Dublin City Council, the National Development Finance Agency and the Department of Environment. All of the officials, both male and female, were formally dressed for the occasion. The two community representatives present on the day were a female tenant of St. Michael's Estate and myself. We were formally present as community members of the St. Michael's Estate Regeneration Board. It struck both of us forcibly that many of the officials present on the panel had never visited St. Michael's Estate nor were they ever likely to do so.

These initial viewings of the various bids were filled with anticipation and expectation. Formally, each of the bids was checked against a compliance check list. Over the course of the morning City Council workers carried in each of the glass encased miniature models and the accompanying paraphernalia for each plan. Each scale model was accompanied by a set of evocatively designed hard cover folders which were contained in a holding case. Each presentation contained one folder with information specifically on finance and one specifically on design. Each plan had been branded with a phrase or slogan in an attempt to give them individualised identities. It was clear that substantial resources had been invested in the production of plans and supporting documentation.

The accountants and valuers present in the room immediately began to assess the financial detail and hardly passed a second glance at the information on design. After each of the plans had been assessed for general compliance with the demands of the RFP, two sub-groups of the panel were set up. One would tackle the financial aspects of each bid while the other would assess the merits of design. The City Council Project Manager for St. Michael's Estate would chair both sub-groups. The community representatives would also be present on both. The finance sub-group was, in effect, led by officials from the National Development Finance Agency (NDFA), and by City Council officials who had responsibility for assessing key financial aspects of the plan. The design sub-group was led by a senior architect from the City Council who was supported by another architect and planner also from the City Council.

READING ARCHITECTURE

Almost all of the design sub-group meetings took place in an elevated board room with an expansive view down upon the river Liffey. A ritual was quickly established for each plan whereby the miniature model and folders were placed on the board table while drawings and architectural boards were placed haphazardly around the walls of the room. For much of the early period of the design sub-group individual members took time moving through each of these forms of presentation. Some would read while others slowly circled round the miniature model trying to make sense of this newly reconfigured landscape. Over the course of a number of days all of the plans were assessed according to the design and architecture criteria set out in the RFP. There were a number of key elements to this including the quality of street patterns, the use and design of open space, aesthetic treatment of buildings, connections to local heritage, energy and sustainability, and the range, type and quality of materials to be used in the construction. Even though the RFP had within it a set of explicit and non-negotiable core demands in that developers had to build a specific number of houses and facilities, clear differences in architectural vision gradually emerged. (All of the bids adhered rigidly to the non-negotiable demands on tenure, heights etc. in the RFP). Each of the plans presented a unique vision for the future estate. No two were alike and each provided a striking variation on the same theme. However, over the course of the assessment process it became clear that some were closer to the job specification than others. A hierarchy gradually emerged amongst all of the plans presented. Each plan was graded according to a marking system which awarded a score out of a possible 100 marks for design. According to the rules of the PPP competition if a plan did not achieve more than 70 marks on design, it was deemed to have failed in its overall bid and was thereby eliminated from the competition. Each of the plans was also given a mark on its proposed timetable (5 per cent of the overall marks) for completion of the project at this point.

THE FINANCIAL STRUCTURING OF PPP

At the first meeting of the financial sub-group of the Assessment Panel it was explained that each of the plans would have to be assessed against a Public Sector Benchmarking (PSB) standard. This standard was the State's estimation as to what it would have cost for the State to do the regeneration project itself. According to an official on the Assessment Panel, the PSB standard was there to 'guarantee that the State got value for money on its asset'. The four key elements to be assessed using the PSB standard were: revenue, costs, project surplus/deficit and developers' "cash offer". PSB estimated the potential revenue that could be generated from the sale of affordable and private housing and commercial facilities in the new development. It also projected the hard (housing/facilities etc.) and soft (landscaping etc.) costs that the development would incur. Costs were then deducted from revenue to see if one was left with a surplus or a deficit on the project. Developers' projections for revenue, costs and surplus/ deficit were then contrasted directly with those of the PSB standard and judged accordingly. Officials on the Assessment Panel described PSB as a test of the robustness of each of the developers' projections as to how real and achievable they were for the project.

As well as testing developers' projections for revenue, costs and surplus/deficit against those of PSB there was also an assessment of each development consortia's "cash offer". The "cash offer" was a sum of money offered by bidders to the City Council after everything else had been taken into account. Once developers had taken into account the cost of providing the housing and facilities required by the State and the revenue they would gain on the sale of private housing they were left with the puzzle as to how much cash they would offer to the City Council. (While the "cash offer" was undoubtedly connected in developers' projections to the surplus/deficit on the project, the figure itself appeared to be completely arbitrary). In conversations during the financial sub-group's deliberations it was felt that developers had mastered the art of taking such risks.

At the St. Michael's Estate Regeneration Board there had been very little discussion as to how the scoring system for finance would actually work. Beyond the fact that 50 per cent of the overall marks would go for finance, there had up until now been no outline as to how this would break down in detail. This only became fully clear at the final meeting of the finance sub-group. Each of the bids would be awarded a score out of a possible 100 marks based on their respective "cash offers".

Marking scheme for Financial aspect

• Best Financial Offer	100
• A lesser bid by >0 and <5m	90
• A lesser bid by >5 and <10m	80
• A lesser bid by >10 and <15m	70
• A lesser bid by >15 and <20m	60
• Other bids	50

(Financial score represents 50 per cent of the overall marks available.)

The best financial offer would therefore get a full 100 marks, i.e. 50 per cent of the overall marks available in the project. Beneath the top offer, a sliding scale operated whereby a plan with a "cash offer" within five million euros of the top offer would receive 90 marks, a plan within ten million of the top offer would receive 80 marks and so on down the scale. The minimum a plan could receive on finance was 50 marks or 25 per cent of the overall marks for the project. The bigger the financial distance between the "cash offers", the bigger the gulf would be in terms of the number of marks given. Each of the bids was assessed using this scale. The "cash offer", therefore, came to be critically important in the overall assessment of the bids. Even though financial robustness and the general financial compliance were important, no specific marks were given for these nor for any other financial component.

Using this system meant that there was a potential difference of 50 marks (25 per cent of the total) between the best and worst "cash offers". The greatest possible distance between plans on design by contrast was 30 marks (15 per cent of the total). When the RFP was originally constructed it had seemed that there was a relatively minor (5 per cent) difference between the design and financial weightings. And yet, primarily due to the gradient scale, it became clear that there was in fact a significant inequality in the weightings whereby finance potentially had a much greater determining influence on the overall outcome than did design. If the design component of the RFP sought to elicit the architectural skills and vision of architects and developers, this was contrasted with a financial component which appeared, as time went on, to be based crudely on money.

Over the course of the assessment process, one of the submitted bids was deemed to be non-compliant according to the criteria set down in the RFP. The remaining three developers' "cash offers" were subsequently marked according to the scoring system above. Just as it did in relation to design, although much more quickly and clearly defined here, a hierarchy emerged between the respective developers. The highest financial offer, as stipulated, was given 100 marks. Those in second and third places were marked by their distance from this in packets of five million euros. At a final meeting of the full assessment panel on 28 November 2006, both sets of scores were added together. Based on the design, finance and timetable criteria set out in the RFP a plan and a Preferred Bidder was chosen by the Assessment Panel for the regeneration of St. Michael's Estate. The developer chosen was McNamara/Castlethorn. In January 2007, all of the material relating to the bid was brought back to the St. Michael's Estate Regeneration Board for approval. The decision of the Assessment Panel was formally endorsed by the Regeneration Board in St. Michael's Estate early in 2007.

THE PROJECT AGREEMENT

Once the bid had been awarded, a formal, legal contract between Dublin City Council and the Preferred Bidder needed to be drawn up and agreed upon. This phase was about contractualising the content of the winning bid into a legal format. In the language of PPP this contract is entitled the 'Project Agreement'. In the Project Agreement for St. Michael's Estate there were two parties to the contract, Dublin City Council and 'Trimera', a subsidiary company set up by McNamara/Castlethorn for the duration of the project. Between the bid being approved and the Project Agreement being formally signed a series of contract negotiations took place in relation to outstanding issues in the bid. Many of these were design issues that had been highlighted by residents, community groups and other members of the Board while examining the content of the plan after the Preferred Bidder had been chosen. There was also the critically significant issue of the level of financial resources which would be devoted to the Social Regeneration of St. Michael's Estate.

The community sector made a formal request at the Regeneration Board that it be a participant in the contract negotiations in the drawing up of the Project Agreement. The City Council rejected the request out of hand and defended its position with much the same logic that it had defended the Assessment Panel. In the end, the contract negotiations took place solely between the City Council and the Preferred Bidder. Rough drafts of the Project Agreement were available to members of the Regeneration Board, but only under very strict conditions. The Project Agreement could only be read within the City Council offices adjacent to St. Michael's Estate and could not be taken away for a thorough analysis. It proved extremely difficult therefore to get a clear understanding of the detail of the Project Agreement.

The two central issues that arose in relation to the Project Agreement revolved around outstanding design questions and the financial resourcing of social regeneration. One of the critical design issues to arise was the energy and sustainability ratings of the new homes on the Estate. Increasing the energy ratings of the new housing would reduce costs for residents and would function as a very direct anti-poverty measure. Over time, a long list of recommendations were put together to deal with all of these outstanding issues. All of these were eventually incorporated into the Project Agreement prior to its official signing. At the same time, an agreement was also reached on the funding of the Social Regeneration of the Estate.

SUMMARY

The Department of the Environment had advocated PPP as the best of all possible regeneration models. From the State's perspective it was the fastest, most efficient and also offered the possibility that the State might make money out of the project. However, the propaganda revealed nothing as to the actual workings of PPP. The experience in St. Michael's Estate would suggest that there were many aspects of the PPP process that were problematic. These included the larger political issues which arise in relation to the housing tenure mix of newly regenerated estates. There were also internal issues within the PPP mechanism itself. These ranged from the different weightings given to finance and design in the RFP, to the fact that critical stages of the PPP process were inaccessible to the community. Had it not been for the community's perseverance and insistence on changing these, they would have remained so. There are many questions which have arisen over the course of this process. In the final chapter I try to deconstruct regeneration and, in doing so, make some sense of it all.

Chapter 10

Deconstructing Regeneration:

Public Good or Private Profit

… to speak a true word is to transform the world.[61]

INTRODUCTION

We can discern quite clearly from the experience in St. Michael's Estate, two very different approaches to regeneration. There is the paradigm preferred by the State and characterised most succinctly in the model of Public Private Partnership. This can be described as the 'market' or the 'for profit' model of regeneration. And then there is the model put forward by tenants and community groups on the Estate which was characterised by the idea that the regeneration of St. Michael's estate should be about providing substantial social housing and a range of accessible public services and facilities. This community-driven approach could be entitled the 'Public Good' model of regeneration, and has at its core the values of equality, democracy, social justice and sustainability. Such values are not merely tokenistic principles, they are especially important in relation to the all too real outcomes of regeneration.

A protracted and intense struggle has taken place in recent years in St. Michael's Estate between these competing paradigms.

Both are very different when it comes to how regeneration takes place and the substantive outcomes which occur. My argument in this conclusion is that regeneration should prioritise 'Public Good' over market or profit considerations. Earlier in this book the point was made that inequality preceded and indeed provided the rationale for the regeneration of St. Michael's Estate. The hope was that regeneration would tackle and change such inequalities. However, within the market-driven approach, this was certainly not the highest priority. In fact, inequality has continued to be a pervasive feature in both the doing and the outcomes of regeneration using PPP. These include inequalities of power, inequalities of respect and recognition, and clear inequalities of resources and outcomes.[62]

In this conclusion I want to analyse the process by which Public Private Partnership was imposed and also to highlight the core objectives behind the model. Then I want to look at the nature and effects of community-based challenges to the PPP model. Such challenges had a profound effect on the ultimate shape of the new estate. The outcomes of regeneration were significantly altered by the fact that such challenges took place. Had they not occurred, the new St. Michael's Estate would have had little or no social housing and minimal public services. It is clear that regeneration can happen in ways which are more democratic, less authoritarian, more just and less exclusive.

SOME CHARACTERISTICS OF THE PPP MODEL:

The power of a man, is his present means, to obtain some future apparent Good.[63]

'Power' (Macht) is the probability that one actor within a social relationship will be in a position to carry out his own will despite resistance.[64]

Power is a means to an end. A state especially possesses formida-

ble powers. Perhaps the greatest of them is its monopoly on legitimate violence. Occasionally it uses such power, but most of the
time it is other, less overt, forms of power that are to the fore. In
the regeneration of St. Michael's Estate it was a less forceful, but
nonetheless effective form of power that was exercised. The
Department of the Environment's recommendation to use PPP
as the mechanism for the regeneration of the Estate in September 2003 encapsulated this power. Prior to this, over two years
work, with Dublin City Council as a primary participant, had
gone into the development of a new masterplan. The content of
this plan very much reflected the desires of those still living on
the Estate. The plan was low-density, and was true to the wishes
of local residents in that it had a majority of social housing, gener-
ous open spaces and community facilities. It was a plan for the
people of St. Michael's Estate. It would have required a relatively
moderate amount of state investment. While there had been a
genuine spirit of collaboration in the development of this plan,
St. Michael's was ultimately to find itself at the mercy of a changing state philosophy in relation to housing.[65] The imposition of
PPP brought with it an acutely market-oriented, privatising logic.

The 'recommendation' from the Department of the Environment to use PPP brought to light a less than subtle
authoritarianism at work in the actions of the Irish State. All
previous work was instantly dismissed and the new policy change
was non-negotiable and not up for discussion or debate. The
State used its position as landlord of St. Michael's Estate to
exercise its powers of ownership, control and authority. The
decision to abandon the original plan highlighted the absolute
lack of respect for those still living and working on the Estate. If
residents of the Estate had expected a state that would honour
commitments, and respect the work done locally, they were
mistaken. They had discovered, as they had many times in the
past, that equality in such relationships was something of a myth.
The changeover to PPP lucidly exposed the power structures of
regeneration. The nature of state power was dictatorial, anti-
dialogical and was very much a 'power over'. It was quite at odds

with the currently fashionable notions of 'active citizenship' and 'participatory democracy'. One side issued commands while the other was expected to subordinately follow. This raised questions about the doing of regeneration and the process through which regeneration would happen. The embryonic beginnings of cooperative community-state relations that had been developing in St. Michael's Estate were stopped in their tracks, even though, from the State's perspective the change in process was eminently altruistic and was done to facilitate a greater good. The transition to PPP highlighted the changing values and objectives that would underpin such a project.

THE MARKET AND THE MARGINALISATION OF SOCIAL HOUSING

The provision and replacement of the social housing stock was to the forefront of residents' minds in 1998 when they agreed to demolition. Gradually however, the State rolled back from this commitment. The use of the PPP model enhanced and consolidated this change of position. PPP is a particular mechanism for achieving specific ends, and while there is a degree of elasticity within the model, such flexibility is minimal and is circumscribed tightly within strict financial parameters. In St. Michael's Estate, two key objectives of PPP for the State were the absolute minimising of social housing and the preclusion of state investment. A third, and perhaps less obvious objective, was the possibility that the PPP could function as a revenue generating device for the City Council itself. These objectives were mutually reinforcing and were highlighted time and again, especially during negotiations. The less social housing and facilities built, the less State investment needed. During meetings officials would often do mental and written arithmetic to see if the model was breaking the Council's financial boundaries. They consistently operated with a working balance sheet for PPP and the phrase 'the project must break even' became something of a mantra. This was code for

not incurring a cost to the State. The possibility that State investment might be needed was anathema to City Council officials
and such a cost could not be countenanced.

The logic of the PPP in St. Michael's Estate worked on the
basis that the State would trade its land in return for the building
of a set number of social and affordable housing units and community facilities by a developer on the site. In return for this the
developer would get to build a set number of private residential
units and commercial retail facilities which they could sell/rent on
the commercial market. As part of the PPP requirements developers were also requested to make a "cash offer" to the State as well
as building the social housing and facilities. The size of such an
offer was left to the discretion of each prospective bidder. This was
the *quid pro quo* of PPP. Using the PPP model left the entire regeneration of St. Michael's Estate dependent on estimations and
projections as to what would happen in the housing market. The
nature of each particular PPP project, therefore, is highly contin-
gent on the economic conditions of the time. St. Michael's Estate,
in common with more and more City Council complexes, reflects
the shift toward the ideology of the "entrepreneurial" city council
as discussed earlier in this book. This practice involves the stripping
down, privatisation and in many cases sale of State assets and
services, a practice which is becoming increasingly prevalent in a
number of diverse fields including health, education and housing.[66]
Communities such as St. Michael's Estate are critical testing sites
for the implementation of this change in policy. In this instance it
is the exploitation of the value of state-owned land which is given
precedence above all other considerations.

The overall regeneration of the Estate, as done through PPP,
became embedded in the necessities and discourse of the
'housing market'. The financing of the entire regeneration project
in St. Michael's Estate became dependent on the prospective sale
of private apartments. All of the physical infrastructure on the
new estate would be built based on the estimation of the profit
to be gained from the sale of these. Logically, the more private
apartments (and the fewer social housing units) allowed on the

site the greater the potential profit margins overall. Inescapably then, social housing was measured negatively against the PPP model on every possible occasion. Providing social housing, according to council officials, had the potential to "make the project marginal" and bring the project into the territory of "deficit". From the State's perspective social housing was almost always viewed as a prohibitive cost. In economic terms, it was portrayed as an albatross around the neck of the project pulling it down. Social housing became a stigmatised and residualised phenomenon due to the nature of the PPP model.

Regeneration as social engineering: From public to private estate

The minimising of social housing was more than an economic issue, it was also, perhaps more importantly, a social one. The original impetus for regeneration came in 1998 when 64 per cent of the tenants of St. Michael's Estate agreed, as part of a formal consultation survey, to have the Estate completely demolished. At this time 270 of the 346 flats on the Estate were occupied. Tenants explicitly expressed their wish that the site would be used primarily for the provision of publicly owned housing. In the *Consultation Document* (1998) C. Morley's profile of the Estate describes a place of severe economic hardship and struggle for families living there. Like many other estates and complexes in the city, the residents of the Estate had suffered multiple deprivations. Some of these were material but others undoubtedly had to do with the abject failure of state institutions to fulfil their statutory functions. Compounding this was the City Council's surrender grant in the mid-1980s which had the paradoxical effect of distorting the social structure on the Estate by removing many of those in stable employment. By the time of Morley's survey in 1998, those who were in employment from the Estate, were generally working in menial, poorly-paid, soul-destroying occupations. On a strictly material register, St. Michael's Estate was a community experiencing extreme structural poverty and deprivation. Outsider perspectives, in the media and elsewhere, reinforced this and ranged from being slightly wary to deeply hostile. These factors undoubtedly contributed to a sense of powerlessness amongst residents living on the Estate.

In statistical terms, social class classifications would routinely place the residents of the Estate in the lower echelons of the class structure. The social class of residents has played a key role in the regeneration of St. Michael's Estate. Ownership or non-ownership of property is at the heart of class identity and class relationships. It is this which generally determines the sort of work a person does, general life chances, educational attainment and consequently, power. Class is also a fundamental dynamic in relations between groups. Furthermore, unequal class structures tend to reproduce inequalities from generation to generation. One of the critical characteristics of those living in St. Michael's Estate, and one which had undoubted effects during regeneration, was the residents' status as 'propertyless' social-housing tenants. The lack of ownership of their properties left tenants particularly exposed to changes in policies and diminished their control over the entire process. The State in many ways exploited this vulnerability for its own ends. It did not act to protect and safeguard such interests either in the present or into the future. Alongside ensuring a profitable development, radically changing the social class structure of the Estate became a core state objective. The State used whatever political, economic or technical means it had at its disposal to achieve this goal. The discourse used to justify such restructuring was that of 'social mix'. As a housing policy, 'social mix' was rarely elaborated on by City Council officials beyond them stating its necessity as a state requirement. However, it is clear that it has deep political implications, especially in relation to equality in housing.

From the State's perspective, the overall balance of housing on the Estate needed to undergo a dramatic reorientation. In Dublin City Council's framework plan for St. Michael's Estate, rejected by the City Council Chamber in September 2004, only 80 out of the proposed 850 housing units were designated for social housing. State officials argued time and again that they were only obliged to house the falling numbers of remaining tenants. The City Council's logic of 'social mix' implied that by placing private housing in a majority position this would transform the social structure and conditions on the Estate. In a strange twist of events, the regeneration of social housing complexes became primarily a vehicle for servicing the needs of private householders moving on to these estates.

What happened in St. Michael's Estate raises the fundamental question: is it the State's function to use and provide state-owned land banks throughout the city for the building of large numbers of private apartments? The restructuring of St. Michael's Estate along tenure lines raises questions about the creation of new forms of distinction and hierarchy within regeneration projects on what were previously state-owned lands. Class and gender undoubtedly reinforced each other in St. Michael's Estate. Gender has been an understated but significant aspect of regeneration. A large proportion of heads of households in St. Michael's Estate were, and still are, women, many of them single parents with children, who found themselves in extremely vulnerable positions. Class and gender have undoubtedly been two of the critically influential factors in regeneration, and are in need of more study and exploration especially in relation to regeneration on a broader city/national scale.

Understanding the connections between power, knowledge and PPP

Once begun, local people and community groups asked how would PPP work? What rights would tenants, residents and community organisations have to information and knowledge of the PPP process? It was clear that certain aspects of the PPP process were far more contentious than others. Gaining participation on the Assessment Panel brought to a head an issue that recurred time and again over the course of regeneration. State officials had argued that the Assessment Panel was non-accessible for tenants or community organisations principally because they were deemed not to have the requisite skills and knowledge for participation.

The Assessment Panel was portrayed as a privileged domain of 'experts'. The State, in effect, was constructing a model of partial disclosure whereby tenants were given access only to certain parts of the process and not to others. Working this way would ensure that community knowledge of the process would always be incomplete and fragmented. The effects of implementing such a strategy would be a community sector working from a severely circumscribed knowledge of PPP. It was only the determination and perseverance of the community of St. Michael's Estate which eventually prised open the lid of PPP by gaining access to the Assessment Panel. Tenants and community organisations successfully argued that they should have a right to participate in the decision to choose the developer for the new estate.

In St. Michael's Estate, community participation at critical stages of PPP was problematic to say the least. Many different rationales were used to justify exclusion. These ranged from confidentiality, to a supposed lack of expertise or knowledge, to the potential legal risks of participation. Once the 'preferred bidder' was chosen this issue arose again as the community was excluded from having any knowledge of the detail of the contract negotiations between the City Council and the 'preferred bidder'.

At the outset, when PPP was being nationally touted as an ideal model for regeneration, it was presented by the State as transparent and entirely accessible and participatory. The reality is that, as the experience in St. Michael's Estate demonstrates, it is completely arbitrary and at the total discretion of state officials as to which stages of PPP are accessible and which are not. The availability of accurate and transparent information on the financial structuring and arrangements for PPP was a critical issue in St. Michael's Estate and is undoubtedly relevant for many other communities undergoing regeneration in Dublin and beyond.

THE ALTERNATIVE MODEL: EQUALITY IN REGENERATION

The idea of equality of condition sets out ... to eliminate major inequalities altogether, or at least massively reduce the current scale of inequality. The key to this much more ambitious agenda is to recognize that inequality is rooted in changing and changeable social structures, and particularly in structures of domination and oppression…equality of condition pays more attention to how people are related, particularly through power relations…equality of condition emphasizes the influence of social factors on people's choices and actions.[67]

I have lived on St. Michael's Estate all my life. I know nothing else. This estate is part of who I am. I want to stay on this land, die on this land. I don't see why we have to sacrifice the space we have already and not be respected for it – or given adequate living accommodation. It is our right to be treated with dignity and respect.[68]

The authority and objectives of the State were not passively accepted by the community of St. Michael's Estate. The power of the State 'over' St. Michael's Estate was never total. The regeneration has been characterised by intense struggle in recent years. This struggle has taken place predominantly at local level but it also spilled out over the edges of the Estate into the wider public/political sphere and on a number of occasions into the national media. The dominant market regeneration paradigm put forward by the State was challenged vigorously by residents and community organisations on the Estate. All of the forces ranged against St. Michael's Estate allied with its own undoubted internal limitations suggest that it should have caved in and acceded to whatever the State was suggesting. One of the reasons why this did not happen and why a spirit of resistance flourished within the Estate had to do with the bringing together of old and new energies within a local community structure.

The importance and power of community development organisation

The establishment of the Community Regeneration Team in St. Michael's Estate early in 2001 was an organic, bottom up response to the issue of regeneration. The Team possessed a potent mixture of experience, youth and spirit. Initially, the Team worked out how to come to terms with the more practical aspects of regeneration. It focussed on building community capacity and getting to grips with the technical and architectural aspects of the process. Even at this early stage, however, it was clear that there were critical differences between the community and the State as to what regeneration would entail and how it would take place. The Team began to understand that regeneration was as much about power and inequality as it was about physical transformation. Understanding and analysing the process at this other, more subliminal level became a key aspect of the work. Over a period of years the Team would attempt to decipher and make sense of how such power worked and in whose interests. There was a constant and unremitting interrogation of regeneration.

As the process changed course, the Team adapted and redirected its energies accordingly. The Team benefited from the value of the multiple intelligences that were present. It developed something of a polyphonic, group-based intelligence that transcended its individual parts. It had at its core a strong egalitarian ethic and was committed to resident participation and education on regeneration. The Team worked as a collective for common ends. Given the constantly changing profile of the Estate this was a difficult task. In purely practical terms the Team committed itself to meeting every Thursday morning for the duration of the process. It has done this without fail since early in 2001. The most basic component of the Team was the core commitment and motivation of a small group of very determined individuals who are living and/or working locally in St. Michael's Estate. The Team was built on the foundations of established grassroots infrastructure and acted as a community leadership structure around regeneration. It developed a shared, group-based creativity and innovation:

> ...innovation always necessarily takes place in common. Such instances of innovation in networks might be thought of as an orchestra with no conductor – an orchestra that through

constant communication determines its own beat and would be thrown off and silenced only by the imposition of a conductor's central authority. We have to rid ourselves of the notion than innovation relies on the genius of an individual. We produce and innovate together only in networks.[69]

A community for itself: principles and practice

The primary function of the regeneration team was to support the local Blocks' Committee and the tenants and residents of St. Michael's Estate. The Team endorsed and supported the position of tenants from 1998 that the land should be used primarily to provide housing for present and future social housing tenants. Hence the title of the community vision document *Past, Present and Future: A Community Vision for St. Michael's Estate* (2002). If regeneration was going to be 'for' anyone it should be for them. They continued to have the greatest needs and such needs should be met. The use of the land was critical in this respect. Central to the community vision was the belief that the 'Retention of the main area of the site be given over for public, local authority housing.' (*Past Present and Future* 2002 : 20) The mythical struggles over land that have taken place in Irish folklore, mythology and literature were just as critical in an urban working class housing estate. An ethical use of the land on the Estate and a democratic process to accompany the regeneration were the bedrock of the community's approach. In contrast to a process that would be characterised by conflict and oppressive power relations, another alternative vision was put forward. This was set out in a number of principles:

> Our overall aim for the regeneration of St. Michael's Estate shall be one where the residents of the Estate are treated with dignity and integrity and are guaranteed quality of life, quality housing, quality services, quality community facilities and amenities within the newly regenerated estate.
> The regeneration shall treat St. Michael's Estate as a community.

The process shall be democratic and inclusive.
The process shall be one of equality between the community
and state agencies. [70]

Residents and the Community Regeneration Team were to find
the realisation of such egalitarian aspirations immensely difficult.
And yet, the value of local organisation became clear with the
State's decision to *recommend* PPP. The directive for PPP and the
subsequent plan developed by the City Council in isolation from
local groups and structures provoked a community-based
campaign. The campaign brought to light many things. Perhaps
the clearest was that even within a context of gross inequality the
community was able to develop a highly articulate counter power
to oppose the State's position. There was something of a revela-
tion in this as the campaign developed and the strategic and
tactical power of communications unfolded. The culmination of
the campaign in a mass public meeting, in July 2004, effectively
killed off any hope that Dublin City Council's new framework
plan would be adopted. The campaign provided the conditions
for the vetoing of this plan in September, 2004. It also adjusted
the asymmetrical balance of power tipping the balance back
towards the community.

New tools for new struggles

Communications came to play a central political and tactical role
in the regeneration of St. Michael's Estate. The imagery and
campaign materials that were developed were the public expression of a whole series of innovations and creativities that had
emerged unexpectedly from the process. With the appropriate
assistance and expertise the campaign had shown a subtlety
which produced tangible material effects. The State did not 'close'
St. Michael's Estate and resort to the expropriation of the
remaining residents into accommodation off-site. Instead, State
officials, while clearly irate, nonetheless returned to the negotiating table soon after their plan had been rejected.

Restoring respect and recognition was a core objective of the campaign. The campaign was in many ways a re-action to the arrogance and authoritarianism of the State. St. Michael's Estate, like many others, was a community in search of respect. The campaign produced a rebalancing of respect, a restoration of sorts. It carved out a space within which the community could legitimately present its own case as to who the beneficiaries should be. It also had a significant effect on public opinion in Inchicore and beyond. At the heart of this was the view that regeneration should have as a priority those who did not and would not have access to the private-housing market. The community prioritised the interests of social-housing tenants and demanded that regeneration should be for and about them. It also prioritised the provision of publicly accessible, world-class community facilities.

The entire negotiating phase was an attempt at resolving these issues. Negotiating the tenure mix of St. Michael's Estate revealed intimately the utterly financial objectives of PPP. The *realpolitik* of regeneration revealed how tightly PPP would compress and restrict social housing and community facilities. The community campaign had altered the nature of the relationships between the community and the State. The disrespect and arrogant dismissal that had characterised the changeover to PPP had taken something of a battering. The atmosphere in negotiations was different and had undoubtedly been affected by what had happened. The outcomes of the negotiations were fundamentally affected by the experience of the campaign. The shape of PPP and especially its internal content, was substantially altered. The doing of PPP also revealed many things, not least the State's interpretation as to how the model would work.

CONCLUSION: BEYOND THE LOCAL

Despite the energy and commitment of all of those living and working in St. Michael's Estate there are clear limitations to locally-based responses to the wider processes of regeneration. St.

Michael's Estate fought tooth and nail for a democratic and egalitarian model of regeneration. But it learned the hard way that the shape and contours of the model had been defined from a distance, within anonymous bureaucracies and boardrooms. The scale of regeneration across the city therefore transcends localised responses. This is because the structural form and conditions for regeneration have been predefined in general. The framework of PPP, where it is used, places strict conditions on what is possible, not just in St. Michael's Estate, but across the city in general. Responding to this generalised social process will require a collective response which can connect local communities in a broader tapestry of understanding and action across the city. If there is to be a sustained and concerted challenge to such inequalities in regeneration, energy needs to be generated in this wider context.

The work of Tenants First is crucial in this respect for it is an attempt to forge connections beyond the local and to join up the dots across the city, and more recently on a national level. It has attempted to 'conscientize' people to the realities of regeneration and enhance the knowledge that communities have already developed. It has begun in its own modest way to deconstruct regeneration and to lay bare what is involved. Much of the work in recent years has been about helping communities make sense of what is happening locally. Communities have come together and shared experiences and stories as to their own situations. Just like the changing landscape of the city, Tenants First is a work in progress. Perhaps its greatest challenge will be to develop a common regeneration agenda amongst working class communities which is egalitarian and which challenges vociferously the insidious inequalities which are a hallmark of regeneration currently.

FINAL THOUGHT

The regeneration of St. Michael's Estate raises many questions. The most fundamental has to do with the deep-rooted inequalities that are endemic to the PPP process as it is structured by the

State. What does it say if communities for whom the regeneration is intended have no control over the mechanism or framework to be used? Is such a framework equitable for urban regeneration? The position taken here is, no, it is not. The experience in St. Michael's Estate shows that the maintenance of hierarchical relations between the State and the community is a hallmark of the entire process. At major and minor moments in the process it was clear that if it was not the State's way, it was no way. If we have learned anything from the regeneration of St Michael's Estate it is that within an inequitable process the outcomes are more likely to favour the powerful party.

The refusal of the State to invest in regeneration projects like St. Michael's Estate undoubtedly has a major impact on the outcome. The dependent relationship of the State on the private sector for the regeneration of publicly-owned housing estates effectively means that only certain outcomes are permissible. The most important of these is the increasing restriction and fragmentation of social housing.

We have, however, also learned from the experience of the regeneration of St. Michael's Estate that, given the support and opportunity, community spirit and resistance can make a difference.

Epilogue

Undoing PPP: Déjà vu

As we turned on to Capel Street Bridge we could see the crowds waiting at City Hall. The organisers demanded that this stage be done in complete silence. Nobody disobeyed. The protest became a cocoon cut off from the rest of the city, suspended in time. Parents and children walked hand in hand. Senses were heightened as everything slowed down. The expressions matched the motif for the protest which was conveyed on a banner in block white text in the phrase 'The Death of Our Hopes and Dreams'. Almost everyone present was dressed entirely in black as the motif of loss became emblematic of the current situation. Two lead drummers played a sonorous funeral march as we crossed the river Liffey. There was a momentary acknowledgement from all of those present that what was happening was unbearable. The silence brought with it a depth and a realisation of the significance of the events which were unfolding. It also heightened the sense of the emotion attached to the collapse of the projects. For a very brief moment there was a collective connection with this loss. All of this was contained within the protest as a theatrical event. But these were not actors playing parts where they could later step off the stage and resume other lives. Their lives and the conditions they would live in were very much at stake. It was a brief but profound moment. And as it passed, it was not just the anxiety and vulnerability or even silent rage, but the dignity of the tenants and their children which was to the fore. As we edged closer to the city hall the silence cracked open and those waiting in front embraced those arriving with open arms and a tumultuous solidarity. The event turned inside out as pots and pans and spoons appeared magically from every sort of holder conceivable. The protest metamorphosed into another form. It became a howling street carnival with a visceral energy. Residents became energised again. Women who had grown up in the complexes came to the balcony of City Hall overlooking Castle Street and said their pieces forcibly and without fear. The optimism and belief returned to the crowd, they ranted and chanted and screamed 'We want our houses'. Chants rose and fell and in the midst of it all, the desire for some sort of justice out of all of this was palpable in the atmosphere. (The Author, City Hall Protest, June 2008)

At 11 am on 19 May 2008 Dublin City Council publicly announced that the Public Private Partnership for St. Michael's Estate with McNamara/Castlethorn would not go ahead as planned. The information was given to the media in the form of a press release and confirmed the worst fears of residents still living on the Estate. There were also four other PPP projects involving the same development consortium that were in the same position. Two of these were also old City Council flat complexes, O'Devaney Gardens and Dominic Street. The other two were on non-occupied publicly owned sites, one on Infirmary Road and one at Convent Lands in Sean McDermott Street. Aware of the potential public relations disaster that was in the making the City Council went directly to the national press with the news on the morning of the 19th.

Dublin City Council confirmed today that the Public Private Partnership which it had with McNamara/Castlethorn in St. Michael's Estate and O'Devaney Gardens, and with McNamaras on Dominic Street, Convent Lands in Sean McDermott Street, and Infirmary Road to regenerate these five areas will not now go ahead as planned.

The current economic climate and the substantial changes that have taken place in the residential housing sector recently, have rendered these projects unviable, from the private partners perspective, as the PPP concept was based partly on the sale of private units to fund the cost of new social and affordable units being provided free to Dublin City Council. Dublin City

Council's priority now is its tenants and the City Council will explore its options for regenerating these areas and providing the social and affordable housing for its tenants. (DCC Press Release to the media, 19 May 2008)

The collapse of the McNamara/Castlethorn bid brought with it an extraordinary sense of *déjà vu* to those living and working in St. Michael's Estate. This was the third time in five years that a plan had collapsed, it wasn't supposed to happen again. Just like the Titanic, PPP was supposed to be unsinkable. The State's propaganda had described it as the model that had everything, it was the most efficient, cheapest, fastest, and perhaps most critically, the 'risk' for the project was to be carried by the developer. At the Regeneration Board, the Assistant City Manager assumed the role of global economic analyst as he explained and interpreted what had happened as part of the fall out from the global credit crisis. He insisted that what had happened wasn't the fault of the City Council and neither was it the fault of the developer. No one, we were told, could have predicted the collapse of the sub prime market and its effect on the economies of the world. PPPs operated in a buoyant and predictable environment but that was gone now. In response to questions as to how one development consortia had won five contracts the answer was that it was simply a case of the best bid having won out in all cases and that all of the bids were subject to the same EU procurement guidelines. PPP 'relied on releasing equity' and the Council and the developer would have benefited from this. But the way things now stacked up the developer would not make a penny. All the City Council could do now was to work to resolve the situation.

Not wanting to be caught out, the other side in this dispute, the private partner in PPP, was also ready very quickly to put their view of the issue into the public sphere. For those extolled for their virtue of being 'risk takers', PPP had suddenly become a risk too far:

The adversely changed circumstances of the current private housing market to that of 2005/2006 when the bids were being submitted, along with the significant additional costs of increased apartment sizes and new energy regulations, have rendered the whole concept of using the sale of private housing units to fund Social and Affordable Housing and Community Services along with a balancing site purchase figure, unsustainable in the current market, despite the best efforts of everyone involved. (Letter from McNamara Construction to Dublin City Council, 19 May 2008)

The collapse of the PPPs provoked phenomenal media interest. It was as if their collapse represented, symbolically at least, one of the harbingers of the end of the Celtic Tiger. The story appeared in newspapers, on radio and on many occasions on the national television station, RTE. One of the unintended consequences of this was a probing of the business interests of the developer Bernard McNamara, head of McNamara Construction, the lead partner in all five collapsed projects. On 25 May 2008, the Sunday Independent carried a front page article with the banner headline 'McNamara, I don't owe 1.5 billion'. The article suggested that McNamara and his companies were heavily indebted to the banks on the basis of outstanding loans and were faced with massive interest repayments. Responding to such negative publicity, Bernard McNamara made a direct phone call to a national radio show on RTE on the same day contradicting the article's content and also saying that he had not, in fact, withdrawn from the projects at all. He argued that it was not him or his company which had caused the collapse of these projects but the bureaucracy of DCC and even the PPP process itself.

The interview revealed little about the fact that there had been months of negotiations to compensate McNamara/Castlethorn for costs incurred in relation to changes in the Project Agreement. Given that the bid had been lodged more than twelve months at this stage, the developer was to have been compensated for costs incurred in a number of key areas. The following is a list of the areas where compensation agreements had been reached between Dublin City Council and McNamara/ Castlethorn prior to the collapse of the PPP project in St. Michael's Estate:

- loss of apartment units due to new housing guidelines
- loss of general build space due to new apartment guidelines
- increased energy standards on first phase of project
- interest rate increases from the awarding of the contract
- construction inflation costs from the awarding of contract

Toward the end of his RTE radio interview, Bernard McNamara philosophised retrospectively and wondered out loud as to the suitability of PPPs for state projects on social housing

> This (PPP) is a very sophisticated, difficult process and is usually only used for major infrastructural projects and I often wonder was it suitable at all for the procurement of public housing.

This change of heart had obviously occurred somewhere in the very recent past, given the sheer number of PPP projects his company had bid for (and won) with Dublin City Council and elsewhere. Contrary to Bernard McNamara's protestations, Mc Namara/Castlethorn did indeed walk away from the PPP project for St. Michael's Estate as well as from the others in O'Devaney Gardens and Dominic Street. After a period of time, Dublin City Council issued a public statement saying that they had reached agreement with McNamara/Castlethorn whereby, they, the contractor, would pay the City Council 1.5 million euros in compensation and would allow the City Council, on licence, to take control and use of the plans that they had submitted in each of the respective PPP projects. This was the official end of the McNamara/Castlethorn bid. Since the collapse of the Mc Namara/Castlethorn bid, discussions have been taking place with the bidder who was placed second in the PPP competition. To date these negotiations have proved inconclusive. The City Council on the back of the PPP debacle has set up a 'Multi-Disciplinary Task Force' charged with coming up with options around the collapse of the projects. Perhaps the most noticeable feature of the Task Force, like the Assessment Panel for PPP, is the exclusion of tenants and community participation from the process. We are back to the situation of the 'expert' knows best.

The final act in the drama has seen the State has make a decisive move in relation to emptying St. Michael's Estate of the remaining families that still reside there. (It is also doing this in O'Devaney Gardens and Dominic Street presently.) All of the remaining tenants have been written to by the City Council informing them that they are now a priority for transfer and 'relocation', while the City Council works out what to do with the Estate. The word 'regeneration' has almost imperceptibly slipped out of use and has now been replaced by the language of 'relocation'. PPP began with a letter of significance and is ending with one too. The Department of the Environment initiated PPP through a written correspondence back in 2003 and now almost five years later, the remaining residents are being informed that 'regeneration', which many of them signed up to in 1998, has now officially become about relocation.

> While Dublin City Council will make every effort to bring about an alternative plan to regenerate this area you can appreciate this will take several years to achieve. In the meantime the Council have a duty to its tenants who remain in the estate to provide the option of moving into good quality homes at a location outside St. Michael's Estate. Tenants who take up this offer will have the option to move back in the future when St. Michael's Estate has undergone its regeneration. (Correspondence to remaining residents of St. Michael's Estate from Dublin City Council, October 2008)

To date, there has been no admission on the State's part that it might have erred in its judgement in using PPP, or that it owes the residents of St. Michael's Estate who have trusted the State an apology. The collapse of the PPP projects is being swept away as another consequence of the global credit crisis. If we believe this version of events, what happened in St. Michael's Estate was accidental, a simple twist of fate, unpredictable and unstoppable. The collapse of the PPP was something akin to a natural disaster. The idea that the mechanism for regeneration might have had a part to play in its own demise is inconceivable. Such a rationale absolves the State and its agencies of all responsibility for the failure. The fact that there had been no underwriting of these projects by the State, no fallback, no insurance or no basic guarantees in the case of such an event happening does not merit a mention. If five projects were so vulnerable and collapsed so quickly does it not raise critical questions or suggest a review is urgently necessary? It would seem not. PPP remains the chosen mechanism for the delivery of various infrastructural projects and in the minds of many in the State, with a little change of luck and when the global credit crisis subsides, it soon will be again for public housing.

As we go to press late in 2008, there are eighteen families left on St. Michael's Estate. These remaining families, such as the Mc Nulty's, the Mc Keever's, the Farrell's, and the Fahey's are now in their tenth year of 'regeneration'. Their children have grown up amidst demolition and dilapidation in a state of suspended animation. To date, they have not seen a brick laid on their new houses or the new Estate. It is difficult to know at this time how many of those remaining will ever be housed on St. Michael's Estate. But to the last, they have continued to fight tooth and nail for a democratic and egalitarian model of regeneration.

Notes

1   *The Greek Myths: Origins of the Gods.* By James Davidson. Foreword by
    Neil MacGregor No. 1 in a Series of 6 Copyright Guardian News and Media
    2008.
2   Brecht, B. (1929) *Das Badence vom Einverständis.*
3   Gerth, H. and Wright Mills, C. (1953), *Character and Social Structure.* New
    York: Harcourt Brace.
4   Rousseau, JJ, *The Social Contract and Discourses.* Translation and Intro-
    duction by G.D.H. Cole J.M. Dent & Sons Ltd, London 1973
5   See Glossary of Terms
6   *Consultation Document on the Future of St. Michael's Estate.* Prepared by
    Morley, C. (1998) Commissioned and published by the St. Michael's Estate
    Task Force.
    In 2001 Dublin Corporation (known to generations of Dubliners as 'The
    Corpo') changed its name to Dublin City Council.' For more information on
    the history of Dublin City Council visit www.dublincity.ie
7   See Glossary of Terms
8   *Past, Present and Future: (2002,) A Community Vision for the Regeneration
    of St. Michael's Estate.* Produced by the St. Michael's Estate regeneration
    Team on behalf of the Blocks' Committee.
9   The Canal Communities Local Drugs Task Force was set up in 1997 as a
    specific response to serious and problematic drug use in the area. The ge-
    ography of the Canal Communities encompasses the communities of Ri-
    alto, Inchicore and Bluebell. Local Drugs Task Forces were set up in thirteen
    areas in Dublin and one in Cork in the mid to late-1990s. They were es-
    tablished to target serious drug use in these areas. Local Drugs Task Forces
    are community/voluntary/statutory structures and are overseen by the Na-
    tional Drugs Strategy Team (NDST) and by the government's Cabinet Sub-
    Committee on Social Inclusion.
10 Corcoran, M.P. "On the Waterfront" (2002), in Corcoran, M.P. and Peillon,
    M. (eds.) *Ireland Unbound: A Turn of the Century Chronicle.* Dublin: IPA
    pp.200-214:200
11 Castells, M. (2004), *The Information Age: Economy, Society and Culture.*
    The Network Society Volume 1. 2004 edition Blackwell Publishing.
12 Bartley B., & K. Treadwell Shine.(2003), 'Competitive City: Governance and
    the Changing Dynamics of Urban Regeneration in Dublin.' in *The Glob-
    alised City: Economic Restructuring and Social Polarisation in European
    Cities.* Moulaert, F. Rodriguez, A. and Swyngedouw, E. (eds) Oxford Uni-
    versity Press 2003.
13 For a thought provoking counter-dominant understanding of the recent

history of the 'Celtic Tiger' see Colin Coulter's essay "The End of Irish History?" (2003), in *The End of Irish History? Critical Reflections on the Celtic Tiger*, Coulter, C. and Coleman, S. (eds) Manchester University Press p.p.145-166:

14   Punch, M. (2004),"Economic Restructuring in Dublin: Global Connections, Local Variations" in Drudy, P.J. and MacLaran, A. (eds.) *Dublin: Economic and Social Trends Vol 4*, The Centre for Urban and Regional Studies, Trinity College Dublin.

15   Myles Wright Planning Strategy: 'The Myles Wright Plan was commissioned by the Irish Government and prepared between the years of 1964 -1967. Wright proposed that the bulk of the anticipated population increase in the region, estimated at 320,000 persons between 1961-83 be accommodated in four new towns located within 10 kilometres of Dublin City. The subsequent Dublin County Council Development Plan (1972) adopted the Wright strategy modified to provide for the development of three towns, Tallaght, Lucan/Clondalkin and Blanchardstown. Cited in *'European Cities, Planning Systems and Property Markets* p.200. Edited by James Berry and Stanley Mc Greal. Published by E & FN Spon 1995

16   McGuirk, P. & MacLaran, A. (2001), "Changing Approaches to Urban Planning in an 'Entrepreneurial City': The Case of Dublin". *European Planning Studies Vol. 9, No.4*, p.441

17   B. Bartley, K. Treadwell Shine, & C. Creamer.(2000), *Urban Redevelopment and Social Polarisation in the City: Governance and the Dynamics of Urban Regeneration in Dublin.* Published/Funded by European Commission: Targeted Economic and Social Research (TSER) Area 111: Research into Social Exclusion and Social integration in Europe. p.12

18   Being left outside this project had a major effect in Dublin City Council repositioning itself and changing its entire orientation to planning and development over the coming years.

19   Study on the Urban Renewal Schemes. Study prepared by KPMG in association with Murray O' Laoire Associates, Architects and Urban Designers Northern Ireland Economic Research Centre. Department of the Environment 1996

20   Bartley, B. and Treadwell Shine, K. (2003), op cit pp.151, 154

21   Davis, M. (1998), "Photographs by Robert Morrow" *City of Quartz: Excavating the Future in Los Angeles.* Pimlico

22   Corcoran, M.P. (2002), op cit pp 200-214

23   Bartley, B. and Treadwell Shine, K. (2003), op cit p.156

24   Study on the Urban Renewal Schemes. Study prepared by KPMG in association with Murray O' Laoire Associates, Architects and Urban Designers Northern Ireland Economic Research Centre. Department of the Environment 1996

25   Study of the Urban Renewal Schemes, Executive Summary op cit p 1.

26   Bartley, B and Treadwell Shine, K. (2003), op cit p 151

27   Bartley, B. and Treadwell Shine, K. (2003) op cit p.156

28   The six areas in Dublin were Ballymun, Kilmainham/Inchicore, North East Inner City, O Connell Street, Liberties/Coombe, Historic Area Rejuvenation Project.

29   McGuirk, P. and MacLaran, A. (2001) Changing Approaches to Urban Plan-

ning in an '"Entrepreneurial" City': The Case of Dublin. *European Planning Studies Vol. 9, No.4*, p.450

30 Liberties Coombe Integrated Area Plan. Dublin City Council 1998.

31 Brudell, P., Hammond, C. and Henry, J (2004) Urban Planning and Regeneration: A Community Perspective. *Journal of Irish Urban Studies* Volume 3 Issue 1 pp 65 – 87:75.

32 Brudell, P. et al (2004), op cit p.77

33 Brudel, P. et al (2004),op cit p.83

34 The Balency et Schuhl system was a French system of production which was made available in Ireland and Great Britain under licence to the British firm Holland, Hannen and Cubitts Ltd. First used in 1949, it had two main distinguishing features which it was claimed made it superior to other systems. The first of these was the use of precast walls and in-situ concrete floors which avoided the need for complex joints. The second distinguishing feature was the 'functional units'. In the Balency system there are two such units which can be arranged to suit any layout. Firstly, there is the 'technical block' which contains the plumbing, water supply, gas pipe work vertical heating mains and the mechanical ventilation duct. The second functional unit is the floor slab containing the heating coils and the electric wiring. It was claimed that the method had numerous advantages in terms of factors such as cost, speed and the number of man hours required. Savings of fifteen percent were predicted on a flat of 750 square feet (70m2) compared with normal construction methods (Building Industry News,30th July 1964). Cited in The development of the Ballymun housing scheme, Dublin 1965 -1969 p. 206 *Irish Geography,* Volume 33(2), 2000, 199-212.Sinéad Power Department of Geography, University of Edinburgh. This article is available on the internet and can be accessed by using the article title.

35 *Past, Present and Future* : *A Community Vision for the Regeneration of St Michael's Estate* (2002), op cit p.3

36 *Consultation Document on the Future of St. Michael's Estate.* Prepared by Morley, C. (1998) op cit pp 29-30.

37 St. Michael's Estate Family Resource Centre Report January to December (1997). p44

38 *Consultation Document on the Future of St. Michael's Estate.* Prepared by Morley, C. (1998) op cit p17

39 *Consultation Document on the Future of St. Michael's Estate.* Prepared by Morley, C. (1998) op cit p16

40 *Consultation Document on the Future of St. Michael's Estate.* Prepared by Morley, C. (1998) op cit pp 36-37

41 Family Resource Centre Annual Report Document January to December 1999 p. 4

42 Family Resource Centre Annual Report Document January to December 1999 p. 4

43 St Michael's Estate Family Resource Centre Annual Report December 2001 p. 12

44 St. Michael's Estate Blocks' Committee Annual Report 1990 – 1991 p.4.

45 *Past, Present and Future: A Community Vision for the Regeneration of St Michael's Estate* op cit p.8

46   Shakespeare W., The Merchant of Venice Act 111 scene 1V *The Complete Works Clarendon Press Oxford:1991*

47   Hardt, M. and Negri, A. (2004)*Multitude: War and Democracy in an Age of Empire*. Hamish Hamilton, An Imprint of Penguin Books pp 133-134.

48   Machiavelli, N. *The Prince*. Penguin Classics 2003 edition.p.9

49   Dillon, B. Changing Partners: How Public Private Partnership has replaced Community Partnership in Urban Regeneration. Causes and Consequences for St. Michael's Estate. February 2004 p.18 Nexus

50   Dillon, B. Changing Partners: How Public Private Partnership has replaced Community Partnership in Urban Regeneration. Causes and Consequences for St. Michael's Estate. February 2004 Nexus p24.

51. Consultation Document on the Future of St. Michael's Estate. Prepared by Morley, C. (1998) op cit p. 12

52   Castells, M. (1983) *The City and the Grassroots: A Cross Cultural Theory of Urban Social Movements*. Edward Arnold Publishers. p.76

53   Community Technical Aid is a long established community development organisation based in the north inner city of Dublin which facilitated public meetings as well as Steering Group meetings of Tenants First for an initial period of time when it first started

54   Discussion report on the possible transfer of ownership of city council rented housing stock. Dublin City Council 2003.

55   Discussion report on the possible transfer of ownership of city council rented housing stock. Dublin City Council 2003. p.6.

56   The Real Guide to Regeneration for Communities.Tenants First 2005

57   *Real Guide* op cit p3

58   This workshop and many others have been facilitated by Community Action Network for Tenants First over the past two to three years. In particular, Cecilia Forestal has had overall responsibility for running and facilitating these workshops.

59   The term 'conscientization' refers to learning to perceive social, political, and economic contradictions and to take action against the oppressive elements of reality.' (Freire, P. *Pedagogy of the Oppressed*, translated by Myra Bergman Ramos, Penguin Books, 1985 Reprinted Edition, p. 15).

A slightly more lengthy exposition of the meaning of 'conscientization' is described in the following passage 'Men, as beings 'in a situation', find themselves rooted in temporal-spatial conditions which mark them and they also mark. They tend to reflect on their own 'situationality' to the extent that it challenges them to act upon it. Men *are* because they *are in* a situation. And they *will be more* the more they not only critically reflect upon their existence but critically act upon it. Reflection upon 'situationality' is reflection upon the very condition of existence: critical thinking through which men discover each other to be 'in a situation'. Only as this situation ceases to present itself as a dense, enveloping reality or a tormenting blind alley, and men come to perceive it as an objective-problematic situation – only then can commitment exist. Men *emerge* from their *submersion* and acquire the ability to *intervene* in reality as it is unveiled. *Intervention* in reality – historical awareness itself – thus represents a step forward from emergence, and results in the 'conscientization' of the situation. 'Conscientization' is the deepening of the attitude of awareness characteristic of all emergence.' (Freire, P. *Pedagogy of the Oppressed*, translated by Myra Bergman Ramos, Penguin Books, 1985 Reprinted Edition, pp 80-81).

60   Marx, K. Capital Volume 1 A Critique of Political Economy. pp 178,179. Penguin Classics 1990 Edition.

61   Friere. P. *Pedagogy of the Oppressed*. p.60 Penguin Books 1985 edition

62   Baker, J. Lynch, K. Cantillon, S. and Walsh, J. (2004), *Equality From Theory to Action*. Palgrave Macmillan

63   Hobbes, T. (2006), *Leviathan* Cambridge University Press. p 62

64   Weber, M. *Economy and Society: An Outline of Interpretive Sociology*. (1978), Roth, G. and Wittich, C. (eds). University of California Press

65   Drudy, PJ. and Punch, M.(2005), *Out of Reach. Inequalities in the Irish Housing System*. TASC at New Island pp25 – 42.

66   Lynch, K. (2006), Neo-Liberalism and Marketisation: The implications for Higher Education. *European Educational Research Journal, Vol. 5 No. 1*

67   Baker, J. et al. (2004) op cit p.33

68   St. Michael's Estate Resident quoted in *Past Present and Future*. A Community Vision for the Regeneration of St. Michael's Estate. St. Michael's Estate Block's Committee 2002.

69   Hardt, M. and Negri, A. (2004*) Multitude: War and Democracy in the Age of Empire*. Hamish Hamilton p 338.

70   *Past, Present and Future: A Community Vision for the Regeneration of St Michael's Estate* op cit p.7